TOP 250
LGBTQ
BOOKS FOR TEENS

Huron Street Press proceeds support the American Library Association in its mission to provide leadership for the development, promotion, and improvement of library and information services and the profession of librarianship to enhance learning and ensure access to information for all.

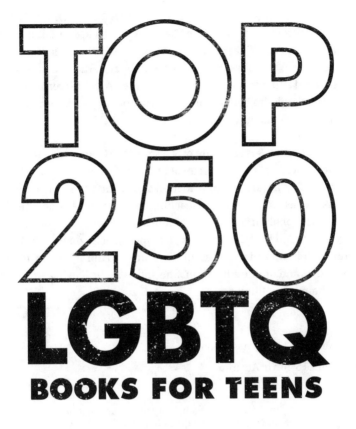

TOP 250 LGBTQ BOOKS FOR TEENS

Coming Out, Being Out, and the Search for Community

MICHAEL CART *and* CHRISTINE A. JENKINS

an imprint of the American Library Association

HURON STREET PRESS

CHICAGO · 2015

A columnist and reviewer for *Booklist* magazine, **MICHAEL CART** is the author or editor of twenty-two books, including *The Heart Has Its Reasons: Young Adult Literature with Gay/Lesbian/Queer Content, 1969–2004*, which he coauthored with Christine A. Jenkins. A past president of both YALSA and ALAN, Cart received the 2000 Grolier Award and was the first recipient of the YALSA/Greenwood Publishing Group Service to Young Adults Achievement Award. Until his relocation to the Midwest, he taught young adult literature at UCLA.

CHRISTINE A. JENKINS is associate professor in the Graduate School of Library and Information Science at the University of Illinois at Urbana–Champaign. She holds a PhD and MS in library and information studies and an MA in children's literature. Jenkins has received several teaching awards and has a decade of experience as a school librarian/media specialist. She is coauthor of *The Heart Has Its Reasons* with Michael Cart and has published articles on historical and contemporary children's and young adult literature and librarianship, intellectual freedom for youth, and online education. She and her wife live in a 100-year-old bungalow in Champaign, Illinois.

———

© 2015 by the American Library Association

Printed in the United States of America

19 18 17 16 15   5 4 3 2 1

Extensive effort has gone into ensuring the reliability of the information in this book; however, the publisher makes no warranty, express or implied, with respect to the material contained herein.

ISBN: 978-1-937589-56-1

Library of Congress Cataloging-in-Publication Data

Cart, Michael.
  Top 250 LGBTQ books for teens : coming out, being out, and the search for community / Michael Cart and Christine A. Jenkins.
      pages   cm
   Includes bibliographical references and index.
   ISBN 978-1-937589-56-1 (paperback)
   1. Homosexuality—Bibliography. 2. Homosexuality—Juvenile literature—Bibliography. 3. Homosexuality—Fiction—Bibliography. 4. Homosexuality—Juvenile fiction—Bibliography. 5. Sexual orientation—Bibliography 6. Sexual minority youth—Books and reading—United States. 7. Teenagers—Books and reading—United States. 8. Libraries—Special collections—Sexual minorities. 9. Young adult literature—Bibliography. I. Jenkins, Christine, 1949– II. Title.
Z7164.H74C37 2015
[HQ76.25]
016.30676'6—dc23   2014031572

Book design by Kim Thornton in the Futura and Tisa Pro typefaces.

♾ This paper meets the requirements of ANSI/NISO Z39.48–1992 (Permanence of Paper)

To Nancy Garden
and the many pioneering authors, editors, and
publishers who have followed in her footsteps
in including LGBTQ content in YA books
and taking a risk to say, "You are not alone."

CONTENTS

ACKNOWLEDGMENTS

W E WOULD LIKE TO THANK CASS MABBOT AND MELISSA HAYES, doctoral students in the Graduate School of Library and Information Science (GSLIS) at the University of Illinois at Urbana-Champaign, for their invaluable assistance throughout the process of identifying, locating, and retrieving the many resources (fiction, graphic novels, and nonfiction, reviews, articles, you name it) that were essential to this project.

We would also like to thank the staff of the *Bulletin* and the Center for Children's Books here at GSLIS: your sharp eyes and unflagging energy made our task easier.

INTRODUCTION

SINCE THE 1969 PUBLICATION OF THE FIRST YA NOVEL WITH LGBTQ content, John Donovan's *I'll Get There. It Better Be Worth the Trip* (Harper & Row), some 700 other titles with such content have appeared. From that number we've selected 250 of what we consider the most notable for inclusion here. Most were published during the past twenty years, from 1994 to the present. In the process of reading and evaluating YA books with LGBTQ content, we've identified a number of trends and innovations.

But first a note on our usage of *LGBTQ* and similar abbreviations: Donovan's book appeared in 1969, the same year as New York City's Stonewall Rebellion, which many view as marking the onset of the gay liberation movement. In the 1980s, "gay" was replaced by "gay and lesbian" or "lesbian and gay" to acknowledge the presence of both women and men in gay organizations (for example, the National Gay Task Force, founded in 1973, became the National Gay and Lesbian Task Force in 1985). By the 1990s, the inclusive initialism of *LGBT* (lesbian, gay, bisexual, and transgender) became a commonly recognized term that encompassed a range of sexual and affectional orientations. Some people add further initials to acknowledge other identities, such as I (for intersex) and A (for asexual or for "straight but not narrow" allies). For our purposes, we have added Q (for questioning) to LGBT to indicate that this book's intended audience includes teens claiming specific sexual identities as well as teens who are questioning traditional assumptions about gender and sexual identity, regardless of their current orientation (or lack thereof).

The decade of the nineties was one of expansion for this literature, the number of titles published—seventy-five—nearly doubled the forty that appeared in the decade of the eighties. Despite this growth, problems remained: for example, in nearly two-thirds of the novels (fifty-one of the seventy-five) the LGBTQ content focused primarily on the coming-out experience—usually told from the perspective of a story's heterosexual protagonist—while relatively few dealt with the realities of already being out. Also, as with the earlier books, the gender imbalance in the literature remained; sixty-nine percent of the decade's LGBTQ books dealt with gay males and only twenty-six percent with lesbians. However, the remaining five percent included both gay and lesbian characters, a radical—and salutary—departure from the previous pattern in which the sexes were strictly segregated. Whether gay or lesbian, however, LGBTQ characters in YA fiction of the nineties moved even further into the background, shifting out of center stage roles and into supporting parts. Complex, fully realized LGBTQ characters were replaced with one-dimensional walk-ons, a trend that looked a lot like tokenism. During the eighties the number of LGBTQ protagonists accounted for forty percent of the novels' characters while sixty percent were in supporting roles. In the nineties, only twenty-seven percent were protagonists while the other seventy-three percent were secondary characters.

Nevertheless, as you'll see from the list that follows, the decade of the nineties was also informed by a number of excellent titles that advanced the literary quality and content of the literature. Characters of color, for example, began appearing, notably in such novels by Jacqueline Woodson as *From the Notebooks of Melanin Sun* (Scholastic, 1995), and *The House You Pass on the Way* (Scholastic, 1997). Latino characters, too, appeared for the first time in R. J. Hamilton's two "Pride Pack" series novels *Who Framed Lorenzo Garcia?* and *The Case of the Missing Mother* (Alyson, 1995), as well as in Gloria Velasquez's *Tommy Stands Alone* (Arte Publico, 1995). Reflecting a general trend in the whole body of YA literature, novels with LGBTQ content previously published in other countries began appearing here, such as Kate Walker's *Peter* (Australia), Paula Boock's *Dare Truth or Promise*, and William Taylor's *The Blue Lawn* (both from New Zealand). In terms of innovation another important nineties novel was Paul Robert Walker's *The Method* (HBJ, 1990), the first LGBTQ novel to include a gay pride parade and a gay restaurant, both indicating that LGBTQ teens didn't need to live in isolation but could be part of a larger community. Meanwhile the first collection of original short stories with LGBTQ content, Marion Dane Bauer's *Am I Blue?* (HarperCollins) appeared in 1994. Another important first followed in 1997 with the publication of M. E. Kerr's *"Hello," I Lied* (HarperCollins), the first novel to feature a self-identified bisexual character. Kerr was ahead of her time; it wasn't until 2011 that the next YA novel with a bisexual character appeared in Alex Sanchez's *Boyfriends with Girlfriends* (Simon & Schuster).

A New Literature for a New Millennium

The turn of the century saw LGBTQ novels graduate from the category of problem novel to that of literary fiction, as evidenced by Ellen Wittlinger's lesbian-themed novel *Hard Love* (Simon & Schuster, 1999), which received a Michael L. Printz Honor Award in 2000 (the Printz is presented to the best YA book of the year, "best" being defined *solely in terms of literary merit* [emphasis added]). This trend was reinforced by Aidan Chambers's gay-themed novel *Postcards from No Man's Land* (Dutton, 2002), which won the 2003 Printz Award. That same year Garret Freymann-Weyr's similarly gay-themed *My Heartbeat* (Houghton Mifflin, 2002) was a Printz Honor title. And, finally, Nancy Garden (*Annie on My Mind*) received the 2003 Margaret A. Edwards Award for lifetime achievement in young adult literature.

The new century continued to see a significant increase in the number of LGBTQ books being published: in the aughts (2000–2009) the number increased from the nineties' total of seventy-five to a strapping 493, self-published novels not included. Many of these were from new small presses. Innovation continued as transgender characters started to appear in YA fiction. First, in short story collections: Francesca Lia Block's *Girl Goddess #9* ((HarperCollins) and in Emma Donoghue's short story "The Welcome" featured in Michael Cart's anthology *Love & Sex* (Simon & Shuster, 2001). And finally in the first novel with a major transgender character, Julie Anne Peters's *Luna* (Little, Brown, 2004), which was short-listed for a National Book Award. Other novels with transgender characters followed, including Ellen Wittlinger's *Parrotfish* (Simon & Schuster, 2007) and Cris Beam's *I Am J* (Little Brown, 2011).

If the first decade of the twenty-first century was one of innovation, it was also one marked by the appearance of a new generation of LGBTQ writers, chief among them David Levithan whose 2003 novel *Boy Meets Boy* (Knopf) imagines an idealized, sweet-spirited world in which gay characters are not only accepted but embraced. Other significant writers in this decade include Christian Burch, Nick Burd, Rachel Cohn, Brent Hartinger, Catherine Ryan Hyde, Steve Kluger, Bill Konigsberg, Malinda Lo, Lauren Myracle, Julie Anne Peters, P. E. Ryan, Sara Ryan, Alex Sanchez, Martin Wilson, and Ellen Wittlinger, among others.

More recently we have begun to see the inclusion of gay and lesbian characters in comics and graphic novels. These range from superheroes (Batwoman) to high school students (Archie's pal Kevin Keller). Altogether we have found some twenty comics (most of them series) with significant LGBTQ content, a fairly modest number but nevertheless a brave beginning.

Speaking of beginnings, as we began the second decade of the twenty-first century, LGBTQ YA books remained a literature in transition. Despite the many gains in the field, further advances are still needed. For example, too many titles, espe-

cially those that remain focused on coming out, continue to treat being homosexual or transgender as a problem or issue. Similarly, there are too few novels
that feature characters whose LGBTQ identity is simply a given, as it is in stories
about heterosexual characters. And in that same vein few novels acknowledge
that homosexuality encompasses more than the sex act, that love is also part of
the equation. Given the increasingly early age at which young people are coming
out, we also need more novels for middle school readers that examine this phe-
nomenon. We also continue to need more LGBTQ novels with characters of color
and characters from other cultures and ethnicities, religions, abilities/disabilities,
and other forms of diversity. Also needed are more novels with same-sex parents
and characters who are bisexual. And, lastly, the genre must continue to come of
age as *literature*.

A Word about Nonfiction

Nonfiction, as well as fiction, is featured in the list that follows. The first nonfiction
title with LGBTQ content aimed at a young adult audience was published in 1979,
one decade after Donovan's *I'll Get There* appeared. The book was Frances Hanckel
and John Cunningham's *A Way of Love, a Way of Life: A Young Person's Introduction to
What It Means to Be Gay* (Lothrop, Lee & Shepard), a groundbreaking work that gar-
nered excellent reviews. But that was then, this is now. A nonfiction title that was
up to date in 1979 now reflects the world of more than thirty years ago, long before
today's teens came into it. With this in mind we have chosen to limit our focus in
this book to texts that will, we hope, stand the test of time. Certainly the subjects
they address are timeless: for example, biography and memoirs, self-help, coming
out, and gay/lesbian parents.

Criteria for Inclusion

With all of this in mind, how did we select the 250 titles that follow? What criteria
did we apply? Well, for starters, as we read our way through the available body of
literature, we looked for originality. We live in an age where nothing succeeds like
imitation. And so authors who bring freshness and innovation to their novels were
shoo-ins for a list like the one that follows. And while we were at it, we left room
for the quirky and offbeat, the sui generis, the novels that appeal to special as well
as general readers. We also looked at character. Have the authors created fully realized, multidimensional characters or are they superficial stereotypes? If the former,
come on down. If the latter, never mind. Stereotypes, of course, have long been the

bane of LGBTQ literature. In an insightful 1983 article ("Out of the Closet But Paying the Price"),[1] Jan Goodman identified ten such stereotypes—formerly common, now less so—that we still see from time to time in twenty-first-century literature:

1. It is still physically dangerous to be gay.
2. Your future is bleak if you are gay.
3. Gay people lead lonely lives, even if they're happy with each other.
4. Gay adults should not be around children because they'll influence them to be homosexual.
5. Something traumatic in a gay person's past makes him or her homosexual.
6. Gay men want to be women and lesbians want to be men.
7. Sex: Don't worry. If you "do it" once, you may not be gay. It may only be a phase.
8. Gay relationships are mysterious.
9. All gays are middle/upper middle class and white.[2]
10. As far as young children know, there's no such thing as a gay person.

To Goodman's ten we would add the ongoing problem of stereotypic characters and situations. After eschewing stereotypes, what about voice? Have the authors found theirs or do they simply echo the voices of authors who have influenced them? If voice is a consideration, so, surely, is style. How have the authors used language in terms of diction, syntax, imagery, and rhythm? And what about mood, tone, and atmosphere? Are they consistent with the thematic content of the stories the authors seek to tell? Contextually, this is the place to nod at setting. There was a time when this consideration took a backseat in young adult books, but that is or should be a thing of the past. A fully realized setting is nearly as important as a fully realized character, and indeed, some settings emerge as de facto characters themselves. To return for a moment to story, what about the plots? Are they interesting, lively, engaging, compelling, or are they derivative, as full of holes as a Swiss cheese, or are they—worst of all—as dull as yesterday's dishwater? What is the book's appeal? Without readers a book is nothing but a dusty artifact. Will these books, then, speak to potential readers? Will they invite emotional as well as intellectual engagement and further invite thought and discussion? Nothing is more exciting than reading a book that is so compelling—or controversial—that it simply demands you talk about it with other readers. And, lastly, do all these elements cohere and come together as an artful whole or do they remain nothing but a collection of disparate elements? If it's the former, look for them on the list that follows.

This has been a very long introduction that should be viewed not as justification but instead as explanation of the means and methods that have shaped the list that follows. We acknowledge that not everyone will agree with every author and title we have included, and surely there will be those who exclaim at omissions, but such disagreements (and, we hope, agreements) are what make lists like the one that follows so much fun. These 250 books are included based on *our* judgment rather than that of some exalted view from on high. That is, we are well aware that different books please different readers, so in choosing *these* books we are not saying that the books *not* included here are unworthy. To wit, we recall two of library science founding father S. R. Ranganathan's five laws: Law 2. "Every reader his [or her] book." and Law 3. "Every book its reader." Sharpen your critical knives if you wish, but even as you do, we hope you will enjoy this annotated list of what we consider to be the best 250 young adult fiction books, graphic novels, and nonfiction books with LGBTQ content of the last twenty years. Here they are.

Notes

1. Jan M. Goodman, "Out of the Closet, But Paying the Price; Lesbian and Gay Characters in Children's Literature," *Council on Interracial Books for Children Bulletin* 14, nos. 3, 4 (1983): 13–15.

2. The first LGBTQ character of color in a YA novel appeared in 1976, with Rosa Guy's *Ruby*; the second appeared fifteen years later in Jacqueline Woodson's 1991 novel *The Dear One*. Since that time, more YA novels with LGBTQ characters of color have appeared in YA fiction, but there are still far too few.

Fiction

**hese 195 fiction titles** include a range of genres, settings, and writing styles. In the early years of YA fiction with LGBTQ content, nearly all were novels that fell into the category of contemporary realism. In more recent years, however, this body of literature has grown to include science fiction, fantasy, historical fiction, action adventure, fairy tale retellings, and short story collections. Most are set in the United States with some in other Anglophone countries (Canada, England, Australia, New Zealand), and a handful are translated and set in non-Anglophone countries. As noted in the introduction, the great majority of protagonists are white, urban/suburban, and middle class, and the majority are male.

In addition to the bibliographic information and evaluative descriptions we've provided for all our Top 250 books, we've also assigned each fiction title one or more codes (HV, GA, QC) to place it in the larger community of young adult literature with LGBTQ content. For a clearer picture of the trends in this literature over time, turn to the appendix: Fiction Codes: Tracking Trends over Time. Here is an abbreviated version of how we interpret our codes:

HV: Most of the early YA novels with LGBTQ content were stories of *Homosexual Visibility* in which a character's homosexuality, previously unknown, became visible to the reader and acknowledged within the world of the story. This revelation may occur at any point in the story with much of the dramatic tension arising from what might happen when the invisible is made visible.

GA: Stories of **Gay Assimilation** assume the existence—at least in the world of the story—of a "melting pot" community of various sexual and gender identities. These stories include people who "just happen to be gay" in the same way that someone "just happens" to be left-handed or red-haired. Their difference from the norm is simply noted and the story continues.

QC: Stories that contain **Queer Consciousness** depict LGBTQ characters within the context of communities of LGBTQ people and their allies, such as a school's gay-straight alliance.

As you will see, the stories that follow may contain one, two, or even three codes apiece. Regardless of the number, however, it is our hope that you will find these novels to be the best the literature has to offer, titles that will appeal to readers of every sexual identity. We trust you will enjoy them.

Books

Adams, S. J.
Sparks
Flux, 2011. 256 p. ISBN: 9780738726762

DEBBIE HAS A SERIOUS CRUSH on her best friend Lisa, but before she can act on it, she meets eccentric Emma and Tim, who have founded a new religion, Bluedaism, aka The Church of Blue. Together the three teens set out on a self-styled "Holy Quest" to rescue Lisa from the clutches of the boring (and seriously religious) Norman who, Debbie fears, is going to have his way with Lisa that very evening. At the same time Debbie plans to come out to Lisa and declare her love for her. Along the way she almost inadvertently manages to fulfill three aspects of her personal Holy Quest: seeing another couple naked, breaking something expensive, and kissing another girl (not Lisa). She also manages to help Emma and Tim realize they're in love with each other. Now will she able to do the same with the elusive Lisa? Though not as funny as it aspires to be, *Sparks* is an amusing read that handles its gay content with gentle—and satisfying—humor. **HV**

Bach, Tamara
Girl from Mars
Groundwood, 2008. 180 p. ISBN: 9780888997258

FIFTEEN-YEAR-OLD MIRIAM regards life in her small German town to be stultifying, the same day in and day out. Worse, perhaps, she regards herself as "every day the same . . . not one thing or the other, neither fish nor fowl. Boring, that's what." This general sense of anomie infects her life and attitude toward it until she meets Laura, a new girl in her class. The two immediately feel a strong but unspoken attraction to each other. As they begin to know each other better, they become friends and then something more as their attraction becomes love. The two begin and consummate a relationship they are determined to keep secret. Perhaps inevitably those closest to them—Laura's friend Philip and Miriam's older brother Dennis—discover the truth but remain nonjudgmental. "It's not a crime," Philip says. Originally published in Germany, *Girl from Mars* is notable for the relentless anomie of its protagonist, which is countered by that welcome shrug of genuine acceptance from her friends as they learn of Miriam's new relationship. Indeed, the emotional distance readers may feel from the characters could be a relief, given the Sturm und Drang often associated with the coming-out process in young adult novels. The book is important as one of the first YA novels in translation with a central focus on LGBTQ content in a non-US setting. **HV**

Bantle, Lee
David Inside Out
Henry Holt, 2009. 184 p. ISBN: 9780805081220

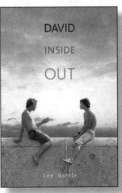

HOW CAN YOU BE YOURSELF when you don't know who that is? Sixteen-year-old David Dahlgren is trying to figure himself out. He's been spending time with a girl, Kick, who is clearly interested in him, but he can't seem to muster the energy to call her for a date. Instead, he seems to be developing a crush on Sean, one of his cross-country teammates, and it appears Sean might be interested in him as well, but David is too anxious to find out. Then, not long after the end of the cross-country season, David finds a mysterious note in his locker that starts, "Want to get it on with a guy?" David's too shy to pursue this lead further, but Sean starts playing a central role in David's sexual fantasies. To cope he devises a self-help plan to set himself straight: (1) Do not look at male bodies! Especially Sean's. (2) No more solo sex, unless you think about girls

... and so on. He even wears a rubber band around his wrist and snaps it when he starts thinking too much about Sean. But then Sean himself appears at his door and initiates sex with David, after which he quickly leaves. Finally, there is Eddie, David's longtime friend, who is openly gay, a fact that worries David: what will people think if they see him and Eddie together. Who says teenage life is simple? This realistic coming out and coming-of-age story has the ring of truth. **HV**

Bauer, A. C. E.
No Castles Here
Random House, 2007. 288 p. ISBN: 9780375839214

ELEVEN-YEAR-OLD AUGIE lives with his single-parent mom in a depressed area of Camden, New Jersey. When his best friend moves away, Augie enters sixth grade expecting a year of loneliness and bullying. At first his fears appear valid, but then his male teacher starts a chorus, which Augie joins, and then he gets a Big Brother, Walter, who is gay. Though at first reluctant to accept Walter for fear that his classmates will discover the man's sexual orientation and step up their bullying, Augie soon finds a strong role model and ally in the man. In the meantime the boy has taken an unauthorized train trip to Philadelphia where he discovers a bookshop and, in it, a magical book that he inadvertently "borrows." The story then alternates between Augie's first-person voice and the voice of the text of the magical book that he reads throughout the course of his school year. The real world intrudes when Augie's school shuts down and he spearheads a movement to restore it. This first novel—combining realism and fantasy—is not only an excellent, well-crafted story, but also one of the few books for middle-grade children to contain gay content. **HV, GA**

Bauer, Marion Dane, ed.
Am I Blue?
HarperCollins, 1994. 284 p. ISBN: 9780064405874

BAUER'S COLLECTION OF SIXTEEN ORIGINAL short stories by leading young adult authors is groundbreaking, the first anthology from a major trade publisher to focus on LGBTQ characters and issues. The featured authors write from both inside and outside the gay experience, and their stories range widely in tone, mood, theme, and content. Some are comic (Bruce

Coville's title story); some are serious (Nancy Garden's "Parents' Night"); most are contemporary; though one, James Cross Giblin's "Three Mondays in July," is set in the past. Most are realistic, but Jane Yolen's fantasy takes readers into another, richly imagined world. Diverse as these stories are, all are moving in their individual ways and feature "literary authority and psychological accuracy" as Bauer writes in her introduction. Twenty years after their publication, these stories are still relevant and speak with heart and authority to a new generation of LGBTQ teens. **HV, GA, QC**

Beam, Cris
I Am J
Little, Brown, 2011. 352 p. ISBN: 9780316053617

THOUGH BORN A GIRL, J (formerly Jessica) knows that he is actually a boy trapped in the wrong body. He attempts to mask his physical identity by binding his breasts and wearing baggy, loose-fitting clothing, but to no avail. His parents and his best friend Melissa— upon whom he has a crush—simply view him as a lesbian with an unfortunate attraction to the heterosexual Melissa. Her rejection makes J all the more determined to speed his transition from F to M. Accordingly, J longs to take testosterone but at seventeen he needs his parents' consent, and he is certain they will never provide it. What to do? There are no easy answers to that question but gradually J begins to find his way. One of the best YA novels with transgender content to date, *I Am J* offers a candid, lucid, and dramatic portrayal of a teen in transition and also of the condition of being transgender. **GA**

Bechard, Margaret
If It Doesn't Kill You
Viking, 1999. 186 p. ISBN: 9780670885473

IT'S THE END OF THE high school football season in Beaverton, Oregon, but Ben Gearhart, fifteen, is already looking forward to next year. As the single star on his lackluster freshman football team, he's hoping to make the varsity squad and carry on his family's football legacy: his grandfather's thirty-year career as coach and his father's three years as quarterback on the school's championship football team. Six months earlier, however,

Ben's closeted father revealed his gay identity to his family and moved out, leaving a shocked wife and an angry son. Ben's father is now living with a male partner and his mother is starting to date, but Ben remains stuck in angry silence, rejecting every overture from his father while grieving a loss he feels but can reveal to no one, certain that his peers would respond with (at best) ridicule and rejection and (at worst) a guilt-by-association assumption that Ben must be gay as well. But then along comes Chynna, a brash new neighbor who is refreshingly unbothered by human difference and who might become a friend Ben can talk to. This book is a brief but memorable story of a traditional guy stepping outside his own comfort zone. **HV**

Belgue, Nancy
Soames on the Range
HarperTrophyCanada, 2006. 204 p.
ISBN: 9780062026712

CISCO IS FIFTEEN WHEN HIS dad, Rocky, the guidance counselor at his high school, comes out of the closet. Cisco (full name: San Francisco Soames—his parents were hippies) does not take the news well, thinking how nice it would be to disappear. Needless to say, this isn't an option, for the local bullies can still see and bully him, especially since Cisco hates sports and likes art and cooking. When one of them attacks him, Cisco is unfairly suspended from school for a week. Then his best friend Karen comes out to him. Then he is accused of assaulting an elderly druggist. All of this happens in one twenty-four-hour period. Yipes! The next thing he knows he's on a plane to British Columbia to live on his uncle's ranch until things cool off—that would be his draft-dodging uncle known in the family as "Uncle Party." Double yipes!! Will Cisco survive the ambient craziness? What will his cooking talent have to do with this? And, most important, will he ever find rapprochement with his father? Belgue's novel is a lighthearted exercise filled more with smiles than laughs but leaves the reader feeling good and sympathetic not only to Cisco but also to Rocky. What more can one ask? **HV**

Berman, Steve, ed.
Speaking Out: LGBTQ Youth Stand Up
Bold Strokes, 2011. 264 p. ISBN: 9781602825666

THOUGH UNEVEN IN QUALITY, THIS collection of thirteen short stories for and about gay, lesbian, bisexual, and transgender teens meets a need for more short stories with LGBTQ content that can be read for pleasure or used in the classroom.

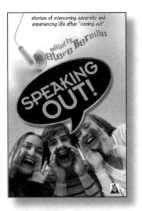

Some of the stories come dangerously close to being didactic and focus more on problems than people, but others are genuinely artful. This collection includes both male and female authors, most of whom are beginning writers who, happily, tend to focus on post-coming-out scenarios and persuasively and dramatically demonstrate that homosexuality is about love and acceptance as well as sex. In addition, each story is preceded by a brief author biography followed by the author's introduction, providing further information about the story's genesis and context. **HV, GA, QC**

Bigelow, Lisa Jenn
Starting from Here
Amazon Children's, 2012. 288 p. ISBN: 9780761462330

HER MOTHER DEAD AND HER trucker father on the road more than at home, Colby is left very much on her own. Too often alone and lonely since her girlfriend left her for a boy (!) the sixteen-year-old finds herself increasingly withdrawing from the world and even from her best friend, Van. When she rescues a three-legged dog that she names Mo, she gradually begins finding redemption and the capacity to once again trust others through loving and caring for him. In the meantime the dog's vet has taken Colby under her wing, and—though remaining closeted—the girl has found a possible new love interest. Making her environment even more relevant to gay teens is the presence at her school of a Rainbow Alliance. First-time novelist Bigelow has written a quiet, psychologically acute portrayal of a young girl learning to deal with her fear of abandonment and opening herself to the possibility of love. **HV, QC**

Black, Jenna

Replica *Tor Teen, 2013. 367 p. ISBN: 9780765333711*

Resistance *(Book 2) Tor Teen, 2014. 368 p. ISBN: 9780765333728*

Revolution *(Book 3) Tor Teen, 2014. 400 p. ISBN: 9780765333735*

WELCOME TO THE CORPORATE STATES of America! New York is owned by Paxco, a corporation that has developed highly prized—and high priced—replicant technology. Nadia Lake, sixteen, is an Executive class beauty heading toward an

arranged marriage to her best friend, Nate, Chairman Heir of Paxco, roguishly handsome, endlessly amusing, and gay. Nate's lover, Kurt, is employed as Nate's valet and body guard. Nadia, Nate, and Kurt have maintained an uneasy balance, but when Nate is found murdered, chief suspect Kurt goes into hiding, and Nadia is being blackmailed to keep her mouth shut. A week later Nate wakes up in a laboratory and realizes he is now a Replica. This eerily gripping dystopic science fiction novel is the first book of the Replica trilogy. Books 2 and 3 take the reader further into the Corporate States, where Paxco's Executive class has the money, Nate, Kurt, and Nadia are on the run, and everyone has a price.

Block, Francesca Lia

Baby Be-Bop

HarperCollins, 1995. 112 p. ISBN: 9780064471763

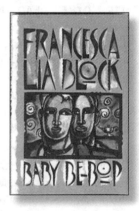

THIS MOVING PREQUEL TO *Weetzie Bat* tells the story of Weetzie's best friend Dirk as a child and teen in the years before he met Weetzie and his true love, Duck. Dirk's parents die when he is small, and he is taken in by his loving Grandma Fifi. He has always been aware of his same-sex attraction ("Dirk had known it since he could remember"), but as he grows older, he learns that the feelings that seem so right to him must be kept secret. His grandmother sees and understands his silent withdrawal and gives him a lamp (yes, the very one that holds *Weetzie Bat's* wish-granting genie) into which he can tell his thus-far unspoken stories. But when he attempts to come out, his closest friend, Pup, rejects him. Dirk longs for oblivion: "I want to be untouchable and beautiful and completely dead inside." When he is attacked and savagely beaten by skinheads, his physical injuries are grave and his spirit is equally damaged. In his anguish, he cries out, "Tell me a story that will make me want to live, because right now I don't want to live. Help me." The help Dirk needs lies within the lamp. As Dirk listens he learns the magical once-upon-a-time stories of the lives of his great-grandmother, his father, and his mother. Mary McCarthy wrote, "We are the hero of our own story." *Baby Be-Bop* is an affirmation of the power of story. **HV, QC**

Block, Francesca Lia

Love in the Time of Global Warming

Henry Holt, 2013. 230 p. ISBN: 9780805096279

LOS ANGELES HAS BEEN DESTROYED by the Earth Shaker and the disastrous tidal wave that followed. Pen's family has vanished in the wake of the two-pronged catastrophe, and narrowly escaping death herself, Pen (short for Penelope) has set off to find them. But could they possibly still be alive? Most of those who survived the Apocalypse have been eaten by a genetically engineered race of giants that have mysteriously appeared following the disaster. But not all humans have perished. Pen soon meets three solitary boys who join her on her odyssey—and, yes, the story is inspired by Homer's epic. The giants, for example, evoke the Cyclops; a former soap opera star turned witch is Circe; there are also sirens, lotus eaters, and more. The result is original and—no surprise—gracefully written. Structurally, it employs flashbacks to fill in the details of Then, the pre-Apocalyptic past. Magic is no stranger to Block's world, nor is her signature poetic sensibility. And love, in its many varieties and forms, including homosexuality, is celebrated, as always. Homer would have been pleased. **GA, QC**

Block, Francesca Lia

Weetzie Bat

Harper & Row, 1989. 88 p. ISBN: 9780060736255

THIS PUNK FAIRY TALE set in contemporary Los Angeles features Weetzie Bat, a straight girl with a bleached-blond flat-top and pink Harlequin sunglasses, and Dirk, a gay boy with a shoe-polish-black Mohawk and a red '55 Pontiac convertible. The author creates a magical yet realistic world for Weetzie and Dirk that includes a wish-granting genie, a cozy Hollywood bungalow, the Tick Tock Tea Room, and their true loves: a blond surfer dude named Duck for Dirk and the mysterious green-eyed My Secret Agent Lover Man for Weetzie. Yet their floating world is no pink cloud utopia, but a reality with divorced and dysfunctional parents, false friends, and painful misunderstandings. Happiness is tinged with pain as loved ones struggle with alcoholism and the terrifying spread of HIV/AIDS during the 1980s. "Love is a dangerous angel, Dirk thought. Especially nowadays." But still, the lovers' destinies are firmly—and happily—intertwined and their world expands as intriguing characters float in and out of the story: Charlie Bat, Vixanne Wigg, Slinkster Dog, Valentine Jah-Love, Witch Baby, and a host of others. Love *is* a dangerous angel, yet still Dirk tells Duck, "We can't be anywhere except together." When this book first appeared, some critics wondered if teen readers would find Weetzie's image-rich urban world engaging or off-putting. Twenty-five years later, *Weetzie Bat* has been claimed by another generation of teen readers. This YA literary milestone is the first title in the author's five-book Dangerous Angels series. Don't miss it! **HV, QC**

Boock, Paula

Dare Truth or Promise

Houghton Mifflin, 1997. 170 p. ISBN: 9780547076171

FIRST PUBLISHED IN NEW ZEALAND, this award-winning young adult novel is told from the perspectives of the star-crossed teenaged lovers. Louie (Louise) and Willa first meet as coworkers at a fast food restaurant and then as classmates at a girls' high school. Louie—outgoing and verbally adept, a school leader, and star of Drama Club productions—lives with her family in an upscale "architectural statement" dream house. Working class Willa, an unconventionally beautiful loner who lives with her mother in an apartment over a bar, is simply looking to get by and graduate so she can pursue her calling as a chef. Although not quite strangers "across a crowded room," the two have an immediate affinity, expressed in their playful rounds of a children's game, Dare Truth or Promise. The electricity between them is vividly described as their friendship deepens into love. Louie asks herself, "Had anything happened at all? Yes, something had happened, the silence in the car told her that." Willa responds in kind: "It felt as if she had come from nowhere, exploding from outer space into Willa's life." Parental displeasure at the girls' growing intimacy fuels increasingly effective efforts to separate the two. Can the rightness of the girls' relationship overcome familial—and social—opposition? Do we need one more story of star-crossed lovers overcoming all obstacles? For this story's finely drawn characters and effectively intertwined narratives, the answer is definitely yes. **HV**

Boyd, Maria
Will
Knopf, 2010. 297 p. ISBN: 9780375862090

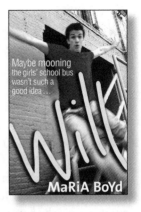

WHEN WILL STUPIDLY MOONS a school bus full of girls, he's tasked to perform a special kind of remedial service to his school: he's to play guitar in the band for the school musical, a production of "The Boyfriend." It's in this context that the lead in the play, Mark, "a good-looking guy who was smart, could sing and dance and play football," comes out to him. Will is startled and reacts badly, panicking and almost literally running away. He then agonizes over his own sexuality, and rather improbably convincing himself that he's gay. His best friend disabuses him of that notion, but can two boys—one straight and one gay—find a way to friendship and genuine trust? Australian author Boyd's first novel is engaging and treats its gay content realistically and its secondary gay character with respect. **GA**

Bray, Libba
Beauty Queens
Delacorte Press, 2011. 396 p. ISBN: 9780439895972

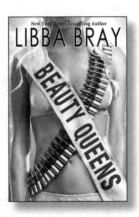

THE FIFTY CONTESTANTS IN THE Miss Teen Dream Pageant find themselves in danger when the plane carrying them to their competition crashes and strands them on a seemingly remote island. How will these latter-day Robinson Crusoes survive? And are they put in further jeopardy when pirates (yes, pirates) make an appearance? And how about the fact that the island, unbeknownst to them, houses a top-secret government facility that is engaged in some extralegal activity? The book's multifaceted LGBTQ content includes a male-to-female transgender Miss Rhode Island, a lesbian Miss Illinois, and a bodacious cross-dressing pirate captain. And some *real* challenges—gigantic killer snakes, flash floods, and protein-rich insect larvae for breakfast (ew!)—await them as well. The antic text is intriguingly enhanced by such non-narrative content as commercial breaks, contestant fact sheets, footnotes, radio broadcasts, and spoofs of reality TV shows. The Printz Award–winning Bray (*Going Bovine*) has written another highly imaginative, laugh-out-loud funny, fictional romp that also invites some serious consideration of feminism and the exploitation of beauty. **HV, GA**

Brett, Catherine

S.P. Likes A.D.

The Women's Press, 1989. 118 p. ISBN: 9780889611429

THE S.P. OF THE TITLE is Stephanie Powell, a ninth-grade girl who is growing increasingly aware of her attraction to a classmate she hardly knows, the green-eyed Anne Delaney. "From the first moment Stephanie had seen her she'd liked her. It was crazy really: to have such a strong feeling for someone she'd barely spoken to. And for a girl." Fortunately, Stephanie has other interests, such as her long-standing passion for pale-ontology, which inspires her entry in a public art design competition: an abstract sculpture composed of replicated dinosaur bones. Her entry wins, but now she faces the challenge of turning her design on paper into a twelve-foot-high sculpture, which will be cast in cement and installed in front of her high school. Eek! Some of Stephanie's classmates (including the ever-oblivious Anne) volunteer to help, but she knows she also needs expert advice on dinosaur skeletal systems. Her mother puts her in touch with Kate, a retired paleontology professor, who invites Stephanie over to discuss her project. Stephanie accepts her offer and is first puzzled and then pleased as she realizes that she is dining in a comfortable home that Kate shares with her longtime partner, Mary. As the sculpture slowly takes shape, Stephanie's awareness of possibilities for her own future expands. Her passion for dinosaur bones could point the way toward a career in science, while her friendship with Kate and Mary makes it clear that long-term happiness is indeed a possibility for a same-sex relationship. **HV**

Brezenoff, Steve

Brooklyn, Burning

Carolrhoda/Lab, 2011. 208 p. ISBN: 9780761375265

HOW IMPORTANT ARE CONSIDERATIONS of sexual preference and gender identity? That's the question Brezenoff poses in his provocative novel that tells the story of teen protagonists Kid and Scout, who meet and fall in love but about whom the author reveals neither gender nor sexual orientation. As Kid's frustrated father declares, "I've got the only kid who doesn't know whether to be straight or gay or a girl or a boy or what." The reader, though intrigued, may also occasionally feel frustrated by these ambiguities and the fact that the plot contains numerous flashbacks. One thing we do know is that the two kids are discovering their love for each other and for music (Kid is a drummer, and Scout a singer/guitar player). Another layer of mystery is revealed when an abandoned—and historic—Brooklyn, New York, warehouse burns and the police suspect that Kid has set the fire. If not, who dunnit? The underlying uncertainties about sexual preference and gender identities are sure to spark spirited discussion both in and out of the classroom. **HV**

Brothers, Meagan
Debbie Harry Sings in French
Holt, 2008. 232 p. ISBN: 9780805080803

WHEN SIXTEEN-YEAR-OLD JOHNNY, a borderline alcoholic, nearly ODs—after a girl slips drugs into his drink—his mother sends him to rehab, where he discovers the music of the band Blondie and singer Debbie Harry. Johnny falls in love with the music and with Debbie Harry herself. Moreover, as he says, "Sometimes I wanna be like her. You know, kind of cool and tough—" "And beautiful?" a friend finishes. "I guess so," Johnny acknowledges. But the post-rehab Johnny still seems out of control, so his mother sends him from their Florida home to live with his Uncle Sam in South Carolina, where he meets Maria and quickly falls in love. There's a problem, though: everyone at the school—including Maria—thinks he's gay. Even the androgynous Johnny wonders about himself, though he knows he loves Maria and she returns his feelings. Discovering that Johnny is fascinated with the way Debbie dresses, Maria persuades him to enter a drag contest. To his surprise he discovers that he enjoys the experience. Can Johnny, a more-or-less straight boy, maintain his loving relationship with Maria *and* simply—and genuinely—enjoy cross-dressing? A well written and emotionally engaging first novel, *Debbie Harry Sings in French* makes an important contribution to LGBT literature as one of the few YA books to deal with the subject of transvestism. **HV**

Burd, Nick
The Vast Fields of Ordinary
Dial, 2009. 309 p. ISBN: 9780803733404

IT'S DADE'S LAST SUMMER AT home before college, and things are looking bleak: his parents' marriage is disintegrating; his mother is self-medicating with pills and

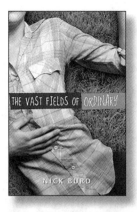

booze; his sorta boyfriend, Pablo, refuses to acknowledge the nature of their "friendship"; the local media are obsessed with the mysterious disappearance of an autistic little girl; and Dade himself is feeling pretty lost and invisible too. But then he meets the dangerous yet fascinating (and unapologetically gay) Alex, and things take a turn for the better . . . for a while. Burd's first novel has some of the trappings of the traditional coming-out-while-coming-of-age story, and the ending seems more willful than artful. That said, Burd is a terrific writer with a special gift for creating teenage characters who are vital, plausible, and always engaging (even when they're being mean and menacing). His take on the complications in Dade's life is sophisticated and thoughtful, especially on the ambiguities of that "relationship" with Pablo, while his limning of the growing friendship with Alex is deeply satisfying, never striking a discordant emotional note. This fine novel was the recipient of the prestigious Lambda Award. **HV**

Calin, Marisa.

Between You & Me

Bloomsbury, 2012. 256 p. ISBN: 9781599907581

SIXTEEN-YEAR-OLD PHYRE is a talented actress who has been cast in the lead role of her school play by the school's charismatic new drama teacher, Mia. Phyre becomes utterly smitten by Mia, obsessing about her endlessly ("I don't know if I want to *be* her or *kiss* her but I know my heart is ready to explode!") to her best friend, who is addressed only as "You." Although You takes the role of supportive best friend seriously, it is clear to the reader that You is actually in love with Phyre. The drama of a story set within the cast and crew of a high school dramatic production is further enhanced by the author's choice to tell this story in screenplay format, which allows "You" to be a character of unspecified gender. When the relationship between the younger woman and her older female mentor predictably falls apart, Phyre begins to realize that her relationship with her best friend has become a romance. If readers are looking for a lesson, the outcome hinges on the question of whether You is male or female. If the former, is this about the ultimate value of heterosexual romance over a same-sex relationship? If the latter, is it about the value of egalitarian peer-to-peer romance over an unequal relationship between an adult and a young adult, regardless of the sexual orientation of either? Readers will have to decide for themselves. **HV**

Cameron, Peter

Someday This Pain
Will Be Useful to You

Farrar/Foster, 2007. 240 p. ISBN: 9780312428167

EIGHTEEN-YEAR-OLD JAMES is perturbed. Though he's been accepted to Brown University, he's not sure he wants to go to college. Instead, he dreams wistfully of buying a small house somewhere in America's heartland—Indiana, perhaps. In the meantime he has a make-work summer job at his mother's Manhattan, New York, art gallery, where he finds himself increasingly drawn to John, an older gallery employee. Uncertain of the best way to proceed, James makes a bad choice and finds himself accused of sexual harassment (gulp). However, this is only one of the painful elements in James's life. There is his fractured family, for example, his ongoing bouts with psychoanalysis, a disastrous trip to the nation's capital, and his general inability to connect with others. Despite all this, James manages, as he tells his story in his own first-person voice, to invest the proceedings with wry—and welcome—humor. Cameron, an established author of adult books, makes an auspicious debut here in the world of young adult literature, writing a crossover book that will appeal to both teens and older young adults. **GA**

Cart, Michael, ed.

How Beautiful the Ordinary:
Twelve Stories of Identity

HarperTeen, 2009. 350 p. ISBN: 9780061154980

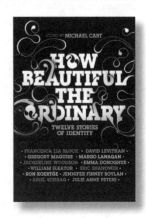

CART HAS ASSEMBLED AND EDITED a collection of twelve original short stories that artfully explore aspects of LGBT identity. Among the book's well-known contributors are David Levithan, Jacqueline Woodson, Gregory Maguire, and Francesca Lia Block. What their stories have in common, Cart writes in his introduction, is their uncommonality, for they demonstrate how wonderfully various and diverse and complex LGBTQ lives can be. Woodson, for example, writes of a young girl who knows what the rest of the world can't: she's really a boy; Maguire, in a novella-length contribution, writes a story that, moving backward and forward in time, introduces readers to a man who confronts his memories of a passionate but "accidental" romance that still resonates in his present-day life. Two of the twelve stories—those by Eric Shanower and Ariel Schrag—are works of graphic fiction that explore, respectively, a (literally) magical love story between two boys and, by contrast, a hilarious look at an ill-conceived San Francisco dyke parade. This distinguished collection was a finalist for the prestigious Lambda Award. **HV, GA, QC**

Cart, Michael, ed.
Love & Sex: Ten Stories of Truth
Simon & Schuster, 2001. 240 p. ISBN: 9780689856686

SENSUALITY—"THOSE PLEASURES so lightly called physical," as French writer Colette noted—is the theme of this remarkable anthology of short stories by noted YA authors. Each story explores some aspect of the myriad connections between love and sex in the lives of teens: Adam and Lily's tepid blind date is electrified by their curious encounter with a ten-foot albino python. A teen describes his ongoing attraction to Matt, a classmate he first noticed at age ten during a slumber party game of strip poker. Two girls hold hands as they share a plate of fries at a diner, their passion stirred as they watch each other across the table. Curtis makes a panicked confession to his girlfriend: last night he dreamed he was a gay porn star—does this mean he's suddenly turned gay? Casey breaks up with her terminally boring boyfriend and then discovers she's pregnant. Luce, who has never had a sexual relationship ("It wasn't that I didn't like the idea of sex . . . I was just picky."), finds herself drawn to the reclusive new resident of her women's collective household. All ten stories are outstanding; four include significant LGBTQ content. **HV, GA**

Cart, Michael
My Father's Scar
Simon & Schuster, 1996. 204 p. ISBN: 9780312181376

A LONELY FRESHMAN IN COLLEGE, nineteen-year-old Andy Logan is coming to terms with his being gay, with having a crush on a flamboyant professor, and with his acrimonious relationship with the professor's teaching assistant Sasha Stevenson. His daily experiences of college life serve as the catalysts for his memories of earlier experiences of growing up and discovering his sexual identity. Prominently featured in his memories are his angry, bigoted father, his gentle, book-loving great-uncle Charles, and football star Billy, his first lover. Also looming large in his memories is an idolized older boy, Evan, who is also gay and becomes the victim of an especially violent attack of gay bashing. Religion plays a large part in Andy's younger life and there, too, he finds animosity directed at homosexuals. Through

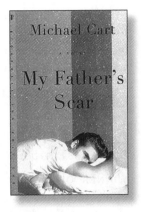

this uneasy process of self-discovery Andy comes to accept his same-sex attraction and—though cruelly rejected by the professor—finds love in an unlikely place. For its time Cart's episodic first novel is notable for its use of a college freshman as the protagonist of a young adult novel. **HV**

Chambers, Aidan

Dance on My Grave: A *Life and a Death in Four Parts, One Hundred and Seventeen Bits, Six Running Reports and Two Press Clippings with a few jokes, a puzzle or three, some footnotes, and a fiasco now and then to help the story along*

Harper & Row, 1982. 253 p. ISBN: 9780810972611

IN DANCE ON MY GRAVE, British author and Printz Award-winner Chambers wrote the first literary novel with LGBT content. Experimental in style, it is the story of the ill-fated romance between two teens, Hal and Barry, which ends tragically with the death of Barry in a motorcycle accident. A common trope in the early days of LGBTQ literature, the death of a gay character is, here, no easy stereotype. The title is a reference to a pact the two make that the survivor of their relationship must dance on the grave of the other. This is only one example of Chambers's careful foreshadowing of the death of Barry, who is obsessed with death. ("You have death on the brain," Hal tells his friend.) If Barry is obsessed with death, Hal is obsessed with understanding. ("That's what you always want, isn't it," Barry says, "to understand?") This reflects Chambers's own cerebral approach to writing, an approach that informs his later, Printz Award–winning title *Postcards from No Man's Land*. If a hallmark of literary fiction is its use of ambiguity, this is certainly an aspect of Chambers's fine novel; it extends even to Hal's feelings for Barry, as he wonders, "Maybe I loved him . . . How do you ever know?" This is one of the most important LGBTQ novels of the 1980s and remains relevant to today's readers. **HV**

Chambers, Aidan

Postcards from No Man's Land

Dutton, 2002. 312 p. ISBN: 9780142401453

WINNER OF BOTH THE PRESTIGIOUS Michael L. Printz Award and Britain's Carnegie Medal, Chambers's elegant novel is the story of seventeen-year-old Jacob who goes from England to Holland to represent his family at a memorial ceremony honoring British soldiers like his late grandfather, who died in Operation Market Garden, the Allies' ill-fated invasion of the Netherlands in the fall of 1944. Once there, Jacob finds himself falling in love both with an androgynous boy named Ton and a girl named Hille. This seems to suggest that Jacob might be bisexual. The Amsterdam setting seems to underscore this; it being a place where, Jacob thinks, "It was as if two surfaces of life, two ways of living rubbed together." Or perhaps it is evocative of a larger issue expressed by the boy's sophisticated, worldly Dutch cousin Daan, who says, "There are no rules about love. Who you love. How many people you can love . . . All the stuff about gender. Male, female, bi, feminist, new man, whatever—it's meaningless. We're beyond that now." Jacob is not so sure, replying, "You are maybe." As for the reader, well . . . it is obviously Chambers's intent to create such uncertainty in the interest of exciting thought and discussion, which this remarkable work of literary fiction is sure to do. **HV, GA, QC**

Charlton-Trujillo, e.E.

Fat Angie

Candlewick Press, 2013. 272 p. ISBN: 9780763661199

"THERE WAS A GIRL. Her name was Angie. She was fat." These simple words begin this well-told and emotionally complex story. Last year Angie's beloved older sister, the tall, beautiful star of the girls' basketball team, graduated from high school, but instead of heading for college on a basketball scholarship, she joined the military. Not long after she shipped out, she was captured in Afghanistan and last seen—blindfolded, bruised, and tied to a chair—on a video gone viral. Now she's presumed dead by all but Angie, who can't bear to imagine a world without her sister. Same school, same town, same family: antisocial brother in therapy with anger issues, disengaged mother having an affair with her brother's therapist, absent father, and no sister. No sister anywhere. Angie is barely there either, more or less invisible to everyone except the bullies who target her as Fat Angie. She's outnumbered, but she can't resist fighting back. Then along comes KC Romance, a new girl in bad-girl garb, a curvy purple heart tattoo on her neck and "eyes that matched her last name." And this beauty is interested in Angie, drawn to her feisty and defiant difference, her refusal to conform. KC's arrival heralds some real changes in Angie's world. No miracles, but yes, it gets better. **HV, QC**

Chbosky, Stephen
The Perks of Being a Wallflower
MTV/Power Books, 1999. 224 p. ISBN: 9781451696196

A NOVEL TOLD IN THE form of letters from fifteen-year-old Charlie to an unknown friend, who may well be the reader. Charlie is entering high school as a disaffected loner, who is making a slow recovery from his best friend's suicide during middle school. He goes largely unnoticed until he is rescued from obscurity by two seniors, Sam (Samantha) and her stepbrother Patrick, who take Charlie under their wings and provide him with the friendship and support he needs to deal with the trauma in his past. When Charlie chances upon Patrick making out with another guy at a party, he is immediately accepting, and when that relationship collapses, he comforts his friend with "You know, Patrick? If I were gay, I'd want to date you." Charlie joins Sam and Patrick's circle of friends as they attend *The Rocky Horror Picture Show* and begins to emerge from isolation and develop confidence in his own ability to connect with others. This book was made into a well-received 2012 movie of the same name, for which Chbosky wrote the screenplay and served as director. **HV, GA**

Clark, Kristin Elizabeth
Freakboy
Farrar, Straus and Giroux, 2013. 448 p. ISBN: 9780374324728

THIS NOVEL IN VERSE BEGINS: "A pronoun is a ghost / of who you really are / short / sharp / harsh / whispering its presence, / taunting your soul." So begins a

story told in three distinct voices. Title character Brendan is a high-achieving student whose teen identity crisis is complicated by personal gender issues. He's a guy, an athlete, with a beautiful girlfriend, Vanessa. But what to do with the pieces of himself that don't fit into society's definition of male? His aroused response to a graceful ballerina leaves him wondering: does he want to *do* her or *be* her? The second voice is Vanessa's, complying with gender norms as she places Brendan at the very center of her world, yet gender-defiant as she competes on the school wrestling team. Finally, there is Angel, a transwoman, with a sense of hope that belies her own lived experience, in which her insistence on presenting as female has meant permanent exile from her family, homelessness, selling her body to support herself, and the ever-present potential threat of physical harm from johns who discover her male body. She finds a safe haven in work at the Willows Teen LGBTQ Center, a counseling and community space for gender-fluid youth, that becomes—directly and indirectly—a healing space for Brendan and for Vanessa. **GA**

Cohen, Joshua C.

Leverage

Speak, 2011. 425 p. ISBN: 9780142420867

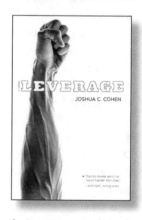

BULLYING AND HOMOPHOBIA LOOM LARGE in this very dark, take-no-prisoners sports novel. The story revolves around the brutal rape by the three cocaptains of the football team of the youngest and weakest member of the school's gymnastics team, who subsequently commits suicide. The story is told from the points of view of Danny, a member of the gymnastics team who secretly witnessed the assault, and Kurt, a member of the football team, who broke it up. Both may pay a price for their attempts at bringing the perpetrators to justice. There is no explicit homosexuality in the book, but gay slurs and homophobia are rife and it is suggested that one of the rapists might be a closeted gay. Beyond this, the book is a sobering and cautionary look at a school and community where football stars are treated like gods who are unassailable so long as their team is winning. Readers of this book may want to also read Robert Lipsyte's equally hard-hitting *Raiders Night*. **HV**

Cohn, Rachel

Cupcake

Simon & Schuster, 2007. 336 p. ISBN: 9781416912194

THE STORY OF CYD CHARISSE, former hellion, depicted in *Gingerbread* (2002) and *Shrimp* (2005), continues in *Cupcake*, this third installment of her saga. She's been living in San Francisco with her mother and trying to negotiate her relationship with her peripatetic surfer boyfriend, Shrimp. After endless wrangling, they've broken up, with Shrimp heading to New Zealand and CC back in New York City to live with her half-brother Danny in his Greenwich Village apartment. Shortly after arriving she falls and breaks her leg, so for her first two months in NYC, her restless body and spirit are confined 24/7 to their walk-up apartment. By the time she is finally castless, she still hasn't figured out (well, let's face it, she hasn't even thought about) what she wants to do with the rest of her life. So when Danny opens a cupcake coffee house, CC jumps at this opportunity to exercise her barista skills. And then Shrimp shows up in NYC and they're back to negotiating the puzzle that is CC and Shrimp, East Coast and West Coast, night and day. . . . Can they manage without each other? Can they manage *with* each other? CC's friends are a mix of orientations, with same-sex-relationship interest coming to the fore as Danny and Aaron, long broken up, now good friends, are embarking on a newly rekindled romance. Can they fashion a future together? Can CC and Shrimp? Stay tuned. **GA**

Cohn, Rachel

Gingerbread

Simon & Schuster, 2002. 172 p. ISBN: 9780689860201

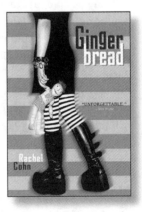

CYD CHARISSE (YES, SHE'S NAMED for the actress/dancer) is in love with a surfer named Shrimp, whom her parents hate. So when she spends nearly all night with him, her parents forbid her to see him. Things go from bad to worse when Shrimp suggests they take a break from their relationship, and things get *really* bad for Cyd when the parents decide it's time for her to get to know her biological father, Frank, so off to New York she goes, accompanied only by her doll Gingerbread. There she meets not only her father but also her half-brother Danny, who is gay and, with his partner, Aaron, owns a café named Village Idiots. Danny and Aaron are sweethearts (in more ways than one!) and hire Cyd to work for them as a barista. In the meantime she meets her half-sister Lisbeth, who is not a sweetheart, and encounters the ex-boyfriend who impregnated her and left her to deal with an abortion alone. Cyd's experiences in New York are cathartic, and she heads back home to San Francisco ready for a fresh start and a reconciliation with Shrimp. Cohn's first book is a funny and heartfelt novel that evokes Francesca Lia Block's *Weetzie Bat* and similarly treats its gay content with love and respect. Fans of *Gingerbread* will want to read its sequels *Shrimp* and *Cupcake*. **GA**

Cohn, Rachel
Very LeFreak
Knopf, 2010. 305 p. ISBN: 9780375857584

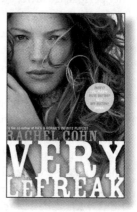

VERY (SHORT FOR VERONICA) LEFREAK, an attractive nineteen-year-old freshman at Columbia University, has a technology problem: she can't make it through an unmediated hour. Despite her addiction to an online world, her roommate Jennifer says, "everyone likes you, wants to be you. Guys fall at your feet." All well and good but Very's grades and relationships are suffering. Even her online inamorato, El Virus, has vanished from the electronic ether. What's a girl to do? Well, following an intervention staged by her friends, Very winds up in rehab at ESCAPE (Emergency Services for Computer-Addicted Persons Everywhere). Will the program help her kick her computer habit? Will she be able to return to Columbia? And where, exactly, is her friendship with her roommate Jennifer heading? Early in the book Very admits to being bisexual—sort of. "Her slut reputation notwithstanding, the truth was she'd only ever been with, *really* been with, four men. Or boys—whatever you wanted to call them. And one and a half girls. . . ." So why is her relationship with Jennifer suddenly so . . . intense? In Very, Cohn has created a fascinating, though occasionally maddening, character whose addiction is only too plausible in this online age. Young readers will find Very and *Very LeFreak* irresistible. **GA**

Cohn, Rachel and David Levithan
Naomi and Ely's No Kiss List
Knopf, 2007. 240 p. ISBN: 9780375844409

NEW YORK UNIVERSITY FRESHMEN and BFFs Naomi and Ely have a list of people whom neither one may kiss, lest their friendship be compromised. But then—

wouldn't you know it?—Ely, who is gay, impulsively kisses Bruce the Second (don't ask), who is Naomi's current boyfriend and is obviously on the list. This brings us to the inevitable good news and bad news. The good news is that Ely now has a boyfriend. The bad news is that his friendship with Naomi suffers a nuclear meltdown. Their forced separation invites Naomi to reexamine their friendship, and she reluctantly comes to realize that she has always imagined that they would eventually become more than friends, even though Ely is gay. The fact that the book is told from multiple points of view may distance some readers from the co-protagonists, but the book is nevertheless hip and witty and will be catnip to the myriad fans of Cohn and Levithan's previous collaboration, *Nick and Nora's Infinite Playlist*. **GA**

Cohn, Rachel and David Levithan
Nick & Norah's Infinite Playlist
Knopf, 2006. 183 p. ISBN: 0375835318

NICK IS THE NONQUEER BASSIST in a queercore band called the Fuck Offs. He and Norah meet cute when he spies his ex girlfriend with a new guy and, hoping to make her jealous, asks Norah to be his girlfriend for five minutes. They then wind up spending most of the night on an epic, music-charged date, which includes encountering a drag queen who is a friend of Norah's. And that's about all of the LGBTQ content the book can

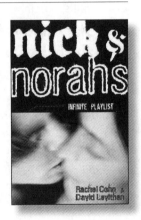

boast. Nevertheless, it's a good read and wildly popular with Cohn and Levithan's legion of fans—especially since Cohn and Levithan tell their story in alternating chapters. The book was made into a popular 2008 movie starring Michael Cera and Kat Dennings. **GA**

Cronn-Mills, Kirstin
Beautiful Music for Ugly Children
Flux, 2012. 288 p. ISBN: 9780738732510

KNOWN CALLOUSLY AT SCHOOL as "that lesbo chick," Liz has a secret: she is a female-to-male transgender, who is just beginning her transition. Though no one at school knows it, Gabe (Liz's male name) has recently gotten a part-time job as

a late-night DJ on the local community radio station. His show, "Beautiful Music for Ugly Children," is fast becoming a cult favorite with the help of his adult neighbor, a music maven who was the first DJ to play an Elvis Presley record on the air. When a girl at school discovers Gabe's secret and outs him, he fears the loss of his fan base. What, he anxiously wonders, would Elvis do? To her credit, Cronn-Mills invests her serious subject with flashes of welcome humor, while treating Gabe and his situation with insight and respect. One of only a handful of YA books to deal with transgender teens, the novel was selected for inclusion on ALA's Rainbow List, a selection of the best LGBTQ books of the year for young adult readers. **HV, QC**

Cronn-Mills, Kirstin

The Sky Always Hears Me and the Hills Don't Mind

Flux, 2009. 281 p. ISBN: 9780738715049

IT'S ANOTHER HOT AUGUST in the small Nebraska town that sixteen-year-old Morgan Callahan calls "Central Nowhere." She's lived all her life in this town where everybody knows everyone else's business, and she can't *wait* to get away for all kinds of reasons, starting with her family. Her father is a mean-mouthed drunk, her stepmother is more or less silent unless she's fighting with her husband, and her two younger brothers just try to stay out of everyone's way. When Morgan is fed up—which is often—she heads for the valley outside of town and shouts, which seems to help ("Today it's *ALIENS, TAKE ME NOW* fifteen times"). Outside her family, Morgan has a good-looking but dull boyfriend, a couple of friends she eats lunch with, and Rob, the cute older guy (he's nineteen!) she works with at the local grocery store. And lately there's also been Tessa, the girl next door, who kisses Morgan one summer night. "Up to that point, I had no idea she liked girls. In Central Nowhere, people don't go there. Boys like girls and girls like them back, and that's all you need to know. The problem was I kissed her back. It felt good. Really, really, really good." Morgan's narrative encompasses a year that challenges her assumptions about her family, her friends, and her future. **HV**

Crutcher, Chris
Athletic Shorts: Six Short Stories
Dell/Laurel-Leaf, 1991. 208 p. ISBN: 9780060507831

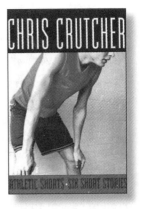

CRUTCHER INTRODUCES EACH OF THE six short stories in this collection with information about the story's context, including connections to other books by the author. Two of the six stories have LGBTQ content. "A Brief Moment in the Life of Angus Bethune" is told by the engaging title character, who has not one but two sets of gay parents, a plus-size body, a talent for snappy patter, and a permanent crush on Melissa Lefevre, the lovely blond girl destined to become the high school's next Snow Ball Queen. "In the Time I Get" is narrated by Louie Banks, protagonist of Crutcher's first novel *Running Loose*. Louie has a summer job cleaning the Buckhorn Bar in his hometown of Trout, Idaho. Darren, twenty-five, the nephew of the bar owner, is spending the summer with his uncle, Louie's boss. The growing friendship between Darren and Louie is nearly derailed when Darren confides that he is gay and has AIDS, which at the time was a death sentence. Louie responds with alarm, and the narrative becomes an exploration of a friendship lost and regained. This is a short story collection with staying power. **HV, GA**

Crutcher, Chris
Ironman
Greenwillow Books, 1995. 297 p. ISBN: 9780060598402

BO MISSES A PASS ON the second day of practice and the coach berates him for not being man enough to play football. "It was our third confrontation of the day, so I told him I was a sissy" (he isn't) "and he was an asshole" (he is), "and I threw down my helmet and headed for the showers." Bo's temper is a problem exacerbated by his authoritarian father's insistence on absolute obedience from his headstrong son. It looks like Bo will be suspended, but his teacher and swim coach, Lionel "Lion" Serbousek—who appeared as one of the teen protagonists in Crutcher's *Stotan!* (1986)—intervenes on Bo's behalf, and Bo is permitted to continue the school year if (and only if) he attends the school's twice weekly anger management group, run by the inimitable teacher/counselor Mr. Nakatani. Bo's involvement challenges him mentally and physically as he confronts the impact of his own homophobia and takes on the athletic challenge of the Yukon Jack Eastern Washington swimming/biking/running triathlon. **HV**

danforth, emily m.

The Miseducation of Cameron Post

HarperCollins, 2012. 480 p. ISBN: 9780062020567

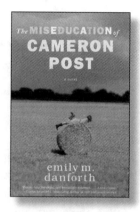

CAMERON'S PARENTS ARE KILLED in a car crash when she is a girl, and she is sent to live with her grandmother and conservative Aunt Ruth. As she grows into her teenage years, she discovers she is a lesbian and begins a clandestine affair with her bisexual best friend, Coley. When their affair is discovered, Coley blames Cameron for their relationship and Aunt Ruth arranges for Cameron to be sent to God's Promise, a church camp that claims to "cure" young people of their homosexuality. Set in eastern Montana, a setting that is vividly realized, the novel then follows Cameron's disturbing experiences at the camp. Such "religious conversion therapy" is rooted in reality; in fact, it has recently been declared to be illegal in the states of California and New Jersey. danforth's coming-of-age novel is a work of literary fiction that is notable for its strong characters and intelligent treatment of its thematic content. It was short-listed for the William C. Morris Award, which is presented annually by ALA's Young Adult Library Services Association (YALSA) for the best first novel of the year. **HV, QC**

De Oliveira, Eddie

Lucky

Scholastic PUSH, 2004. 239 p. ISBN: 9780439546553

SET IN ENGLAND, BRITISH AUTHOR De Oliveira's often amusing first novel is the story of nineteen-year-old, soccer-playing Sam Smith, who has just finished his first year of college and is confused about his sexual identity. He likes girls but, he tentatively admits, "I might possibly in effect maybe potentially have the capacity to fancy boys." Then he meets Toby, another soccer player, and feels a powerful attraction to the boy ("The sexual tension was unbearable"). Toby, who is bisexual, introduces him to gay nightlife in London but Sam remains uncertain ("My state of mind was as tangled as a bowl of spaghetti") and—if he is gay—terrified of being found out by his soccer teammates ("I reasoned that the whole team would be calling me 'bum bandit' by the end of the next training session"). After a summer full of reflection, Sam realizes he must come to terms with his sexual identity. But what is it? Might he be gay or bisexual like Toby? No spoilers here, but the fact is, this is one of only a handful of LGBTQ books to feature, in Sam's friend Toby, a bisexual character and, happily, an appealing one to boot. Other novels about bisexuality include Alex Sanchez' *Boyfriends with Girlfriends* and M. E. Kerr's *"Hello," I Lied*. **HV**

Diaz, Alexandra

Of All the Stupid Things

Egmont, 2010. 258 p. ISBN: 9781606840344

OH, THOSE RUMORS. This one is especially awful: that Tara's hunky boyfriend Brent has slept with a cheerleader—a male cheerleader. Not knowing what to believe, Tara takes a time-out from the relationship. And then, wouldn't you just know it, a new girl comes to town, beautiful Riley with that waist-length black hair, and Tara finds herself falling in love. In the meantime her nearly lifelong friendship with Whitney and Pinkie begins to unravel, not helped by the new rumors about Tara. Soon they're more than rumors as Tara comes out to her Mom (who takes it well) and, making no secret of her feelings for Riley, unofficially outs herself at school. Whitney does not take this news kindly; Pinkie is more ambiguous; as for the rest of the kids at school, they seem to be largely indifferent. The story's point of view rotates among the three girls, so the book is not exclusively focused on Tara, though she is arguably the protagonist and what happens to her in both of her relationships will be the focus of the reader's attention in this middling successful romance. Give it an E for effort and a B for content. **HV**

Dole, Mayra Lazara

Down to the Bone

HarperTeen, 2008. 367 p. ISBN: 9780060843106

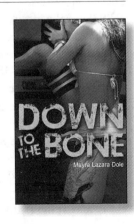

ON THE EVE OF HER second anniversary with Marlena, the love of her life, Cuban-American Laura is outed when her teacher discovers a love letter from Marlena and reads it aloud to her parochial school class. As a result, "the psycho nuns from hell" expel her. And then her hysterical mother calls her "abnormal" and kicks her out of their home in Miami's Little Havana. Fortunately, Laura is invited to move in with her best friend, Soli, and her mother. But unfortunately, Marlena's family sends her back to Puerto Rico, where she is to be married. Desolate, Laura decides—against her friends' protests—to follow Marlena's strategy and start dating a man to pacify her militant mother. But then she meets Gisela. . . . Dole's exuberant novel is notable for its Latina protagonist—a rarity in LGBT literature—and for its depiction of Cuban life and culture, including its censorious attitudes toward homosexuality. Despite this and Laura's difficulties in coming to terms with her homosexuality, the novel is often funny and always highly energetic, even manic. There are many gay characters in the book and, notably—in Tazer—a female-to-male transgender character. They are, without exception, vividly portrayed and come alive on the page, ensuring that *Down to the Bone* is downright delightful. **HV**

Donoghue, Emma

Kissing the Witch: Old Tales in New Skins

HarperCollins, 1997. 240 p. ISBN: 9780064407724.

A HAUNTING AND BRILLIANTLY CONCEIVED collection of thirteen interconnected fairy tales, each tale is recognizable yet new—told from the perspective of the heroine herself. Snow White, Sleeping Beauty, Rapunzel, and other heroines finally have their say. The collection begins with Cinderella's narrative, *The Story of the Shoe*: "Till she came it was all cold. Ever since my mother died the feather bed felt hard as a stone floor. Every word that came out of my mouth limped away like a toad. . . . I scrubbed and swept because there was nothing else to do." There is no cruel stepmother or stepsisters here, just an endless solitude finally interrupted by a strange and beautiful fairy godmother. "I thought for a moment she must have come out of the fire. Her eyes had flames in their centers, and her eyebrows were silvered with ash." The stranger's arrival heralds a new life for the narrator—dresses, coaches, balls, and, yes, a prince—but is this in fact her happy ending? No. The girl considers but wisely rejects the pallid future proposed by the prince in favor of the unconventional but far happier ending she finds in the loving embrace of that beautiful stranger, her fairy godmother. "In the morning I asked, Who were you before you walked into my kitchen? And she said, Will I tell you my own story? It is the tale of a bird," and so begins the next story, narrated by the reimagined fairy godmother: "When I was as young as you are now I learned how to save my own life." Donoghue's audacious stories challenge readers to take a closer look at the well-known fairy tales that shape our lives. **GA**

Eagland, Jane
Wildthorn
Houghton Mifflin, 2010. 350 p. ISBN: 9780547370170

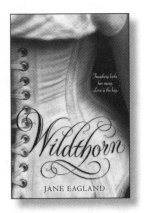

THINKING SHE IS BEING SENT to serve as a companion to the wealthy Woodville family's eldest daughter, seventeen-year-old Louisa Cosgrove finds herself, instead, remanded to Wildthorn Hall, an asylum for the insane. But why, since she's not ill? Flashback eleven years: we see the then-six-year-old Louisa stoutly asserting that when she grows up, she doesn't want to marry; *she* wants to be a scientist despite the fact that both ambitions are anathema to her Victorian England world. In successive flashbacks we see her views remain stubbornly constant as her desire for independence grows except she tweaks her career goal: she now wants to become a doctor like her late father. Are these "insane" views the reason for her being sent to Wildthorn Hall, and do they have something to do with her undeclared love for her beautiful cousin Grace? A better question is how will she survive the hellish conditions at the asylum, where the only bright spot in her miserable existence there is the attendant Eliza. As time passes, Louisa finds her affection for Eliza growing. Might it be her salvation? Eagland's plot-rich novel takes readers into the nightmarish world of the nineteenth-century treatment of the mentally ill while also exposing the unenlightened treatment of women in Victorian society. Her sympathetic treatment of homosexuality is believably consistent with societal views of the time. An altogether excellent novel. **HV**

Farizan, Sara
If You Could Be Mine
Algonquin Young Readers, 2013. 256 p.
ISBN: 9781616202514

SAHAR AND NASRIN HAVE BEEN in love since they were little girls. But how can they possibly enjoy a life together? They live in Iran where homosexuality is considered a crime that may be punishable by death. Things take a turn for the worse when Nasrin's traditional parents—ignorant of their daughter's sexual orientation—arrange a marriage for her. What to do? Sahar comes up with a desperate plan: she will have sexual reassignment surgery, becoming a man so the two girls can marry. Interestingly, such surgery is not illegal in Iran; indeed, the government has even funded it. But is it the answer to Sahar and Nasrin's plight, and if so, will Sahar—even with the loving support of a transsexual friend—be able to follow through? First-time novelist Farizan has written a fascinating and compassionate account of two girls' love in the well-realized context of clandestine gay life in contemporary Iran. **HV**

Farrey, Brian
With or Without You
Simon & Schuster, 2011. 368 p. ISBN: 9781442406995

HAVING GRADUATED FROM HIGH SCHOOL, teenage best friends Evan and Davis are looking forward to attending the University of Chicago in the fall. In the meantime, weary of being bullied and abused for their homosexuality, the two discover a local gay support group called Chasers and enthusiastically join, looking for community and a common purpose. They soon learn, however, that the organization has more sinister aims, including "bug chasing" (i.e., purposely attempting to catch AIDS). It will be up to Evan to extricate Davis, who has become a true believer, from the Chasers. Though this first novel has its flaws—the writing tends to be overintellectualized—it is not without drama and, in Evan and Davis, it boasts sympathetic characters who invite readers' empathy. The novel is also important for its treatment of AIDS, one of the few recent novels to deal with this important subject. A brief afterword offers further information about the disease and references to additional material. **GA, QC**

Federle, Tim
Better Nate than Ever
Simon & Schuster Books for Young Readers, 2013. 275 p. ISBN: 9781442446892

NATE FOSTER, A THIRTEEN-YEAR-OLD with talent, pluck, and a passion for show tunes, has stagestruck ambitions that can't be accommodated in his hometown of Janksburg, Pennsylvania. When he learns that *E.T. The Musical* is in the works for a Broadway run and that open auditions are coming up soon (like, next week!), he decides that his longing for the Great White

Way can no longer be denied. With the help of his best friend, Libby, he makes plans to hop on an eastbound Greyhound bus, zip in to NYC, audition, and then zip out before his parents even realize he's gone (uh-huh . . .). He arrives at Penn Station, finds his way to the theatre and, yes, right into the audition! Does he get a call back? How soon before his cell phone dies? How long will it take his parents to figure out he's gone? How soon will Libby spill the beans? Nate's buoyant spirit shines on every page, and it's immensely refreshing to read his confident understanding that, despite the narrow-minded views and limited dreams of most of his middle school classmates, there really is a big and amazing world outside his hometown, and he can get there, not quite yet perhaps, but soon. **HV**

Ferris, Jean
Eight Seconds
Harcourt, Inc., 2000. 186 p. ISBN: 9780152023676

SET IN THE CURRENT-DAY AMERICAN West, Ferris's exceptionally fine novel is the story of eighteen-year-old John's sometimes painful coming-of-age. While spending five days at a rodeo camp, John meets Kit, a handsome, mature older boy. The two quickly become friends, but when John discovers Kit is gay, things become, well, awkward. John has always felt different; serious heart surgery in childhood put him a year behind in school, but the difference he now feels when he thinks about Kit is more emotionally difficult. And to his dismay, he finds he is afraid to be seen in public with his new friend, fearing people will get "the wrong idea" about him. But will it be the wrong idea? John doesn't know; but his strong attraction to Kit feels like more than friendship, maybe a chemistry that he hasn't experienced before. Ferris does a beautiful job of dramatizing John's gradually evolving self-understanding and—in Kit—of creating a paradigmatically self-aware and emotionally mature gay teenager. Readers will hope that John might find the strength to "cowboy up" and come to terms with his innermost feelings and pursue a future with Kit. But Ferris is wise enough to acknowledge that life is not always about simple happy endings but, instead, about evolving self-knowledge that promises future wisdom. In the process she has written one of the finest contemporary LGBT novels. **HV**

Ford, Michael Thomas
Suicide Notes
HarperTeen, 2008. 295 p. ISBN: 9780060737559

ACCORDING TO FORD, ABOUT a third of gay young people attempt suicide. Jeff is one of these. His first-person narrative begins as he awakens one morning and finds himself in the psychiatric ward of a hospital. His initial response is disbelief. "I'm not crazy," he says. "I don't see what the big deal is about what happened." But, of course, attempting suicide *is* a big deal as he discovers upon learning that he will be spending the next forty-five days in the hospital's in-patient adolescent treatment program. He is resolutely determined not to cooperate with the unit psychiatrist, answering the doctor's questions with sarcasm (and occasional wit), and adamantly refusing to tell him—or the reader—why he attempted suicide. But slowly, gradually, he begins to open up and finally acknowledges his own truth: he is gay. But is that the reason for his suicide attempt? Or is there yet another secret, this one more dramatic? In the meantime Jeff must finally begin to deal with his sexual identity. With the doctor's help, he makes his first tentative steps in that direction, coming out to his parents. Their response is inconclusive, but there appears to be hope for a healthy future. Though suicide attempts are not uncommon in LGBTQ literature, Ford's take on the subject is compassionate and believable without histrionics. This discussable book includes an appendix of information about teen suicide prevention. **HV**

Franklin, Emily and Brendan Halpin
Tessa Masterson Will Go to Prom
Walker, 2012. 257 p. ISBN: 9780802723451

TESSA AND LUCAS HAVE BEEN best friends forever—that and nothing more, just friends—until Lucas starts thinking he'd like their relationship to be something more, something, well, romantic. And so he decides to invite Tessa to prom in a very, er, romantic way: he posts the invitation on a twenty-foot high billboard. Tessa's reaction is unexpected to say the least: she comes out as a lesbian and is determined to go to prom but with her girlfriend while wearing a tux. Lucas doesn't react well to the news; he's furious that Tessa hasn't told him her secret earlier. Then, thinking she has told others, he inadvertently outs her at the same time she is coming out to her parents. From there things become increasingly uncomfortable for both Tessa and Lucas and increasingly public. The thought of a girl taking another girl to prom inflames the small Indiana community's passions, and protestors descend on the school, attracting national attention. What will happen? Will Tessa go to prom? Will the event be canceled? Will Tessa and Lucas reconcile? Coauthors Franklin and Halpin provide answers in a novel (told from Tessa and Lucas's respective points of view) that manages to be accessible even as it examines serious, ripped-from-the-headlines issues regarding gay rights. **GA**

Frazer, Megan
Secrets of Truth & Beauty
Disney/Hyperion, 2009. 347 p. ISBN: 9781423117117

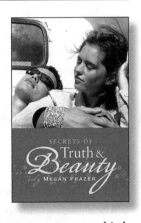

SEVENTEEN-YEAR-OLD DARA COHEN IS A classic example of a girl with "such a pretty face" and a plus-sized body. The high point of her life is now ten years in the past, when she won the title of "Little Miss Maine" by belting out Ella Fitzgerald's jazz version of "A Tisket, A Tasket" while tap dancing. But in the intervening years, "It just sort of happened, right around the time I turned eleven. First the hips came, and then the boobs. . . . I was too big for regular girls' sizes." Then one day Dara comes across a birth certificate for "Rachel Cohen" in her mother's filing cabinet and is astounded to learn that she has an older sister. When she confronts her parents, they tell her that Rachel was a rebellious misfit who left home and cut all family ties the year before Dara was born. Her parents think she might be living somewhere in western Massachusetts, but they are certain that that their mutual estrangement is permanent. End of story. Or is it? Dara's term project in English is a multimedia autobiography; hers opens with video footage of her Little Miss Maine performance followed by a collage of words and images documenting her struggles as a large-bodied girl in a society that places a high value on thinness. When her teacher and parents find her work incomprehensible, Dara does the unthinkable when she tracks down and contacts her sister, now living on a farm with her intentional family of friends and a herd of dairy goats. With a startled Rachel's agreement, Dara spends an improbable and revelatory summer living with her sister, an out lesbian, on Jezebel Goat Farm, once a refuge for young lesbians rejected by their families and now home to an increasingly successful artisanal goat cheese business. **GA**

Freymann-Weyr, Garret
My Heartbeat
Houghton Mifflin, 2002. 154 p. ISBN: 9780618141814

FOURTEEN-YEAR-OLD ELLEN is "totally, madly in love" with her older brother Link's best friend, James. When a girl at school innocently asks if the two boys are a couple, a surprised and disturbed Ellen decides to ask them. "I'm not gay," Link snaps. "James is gay." While the simple question and Link's visceral reaction threaten to destroy the boys' friendship, James and Ellen remain close; indeed, although James acknowledges having slept with men, the two fall in love and, in a nonexplicit sex scene, consummate their relationship. Freymann-Weyr's Printz Honor Award novel is a study in the ambiguities and complexities of sexual identity. That is, James may be perceived as bisexual but does Link protest too much? Why is he willing to accept money from his father to date a girl? What is he afraid of? Is he actually gay? Expect no easy answers from this character-driven work of literary fiction but, instead, an abundance of questions that invite readers to provide their own answers. **HV**

Garden, Nancy
Annie on My Mind
Farrar, Straus and Giroux, 1982. 263 p.
ISBN: 9780374400118

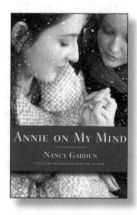

GARDEN'S NOVEL, FIRST PUBLISHED IN 1982, has become a classic of young adult literature, the first lesbian love story with a happy ending. Pre-*Annie*, YA novels with LGBTQ content had treated homosexuality as little more than a problematic—and temporary—form of sexual exploration. Garden changed all that by portraying the emerging relationship between her teenage protagonists, Liza and Annie, as they fall in love. Meeting at the Metropolitan Museum of Art, the two girls experience an instant kinship, a feeling that gradually and believably develops into something more emotionally multilayered and complex. Circumstances at Liza's school conspire to destroy the girls' relationship, but can the bond between them be broken? In the face of adversity, Liza and Annie must struggle separately to maintain their belief in each other and their hope that sometimes love—not ignorance—can win. Viewed in retrospect, some parts of the novel may seem melodramatic, the treatment of its antagonists a bit one-dimensional, but the emotional content remains vividly realized, authentic, and relevant to the questioning hearts of today's teens. This novel justifiably earned Garden the 2003 Margaret A. Edwards Award for Lifetime Achievement in Young Adult Literature. **HV**

Geerling, Marjetta
Fancy White Trash
Viking, 2008. 257 p. ISBN: 9780670010820

ABBY HAS DECIDED THAT THERE are five rules to falling in love; together they comprise her One True Love Plan. Her goal is to avoid the soap operatic mistakes of the heart her mother and older sisters have made—mistakes that have made them "fancy white trash" in the eyes of nearly everyone in their community. For just one example, her sister is sleeping with her stepfather while her mother is pregnant with his baby. No wonder Abby thinks her family belongs on the reality TV show *Jerry Springer*. Is it ultimately better, though, to follow your heart rather than follow the rules? That's the question Abby asks herself vis-à-vis the older boy next door, who may or may not be the father of her unwed sister's baby. Accordingly she struggles mightily not to fall in love with him. Meanwhile his younger brother, Abby's best friend, is gay but afraid to come out of the closet. Using her rules, Abby decides she can at least find his One True Love. Needless to say, complications—many complications—ensue, not all of them fortunate. Author Geerling claims to be a soap opera addict, and she certainly brings that sensibility to her first novel, which is filled with emotional Sturm und Drang and, yes, follows many an emotional vicissitude to offer a happy, emotionally satisfying ending. **HV**

Gennari, Jennifer
My Mixed-Up Berry Blue Summer
Houghton Mifflin, 2012. 119 p. ISBN: 9780547577395

IT'S SUMMER IN VERMONT and twelve-year-old June dreams of entering a winning pie in the Champlain Valley Fair. She can see the headline already: "Wild Berry Pie by June Farrell, 12, Astonishes Judges." Unfortunately, the real headlines are all about a statewide ballot initiative to repeal the state's civil union law. For June this strikes dangerously close to home because she has two mothers: her birth mother, MJ, and her mother's partner, Eva. June is often annoyed by the punctilious Eva, and she *hates* the ugly teasing and taunts that have become part of her daily life. And if MJ and Eva go through with their plans to marry in a civil ceremony, she's certain there'll be worse. Gennari has written a gentle book about a politically contentious subject, the Take Back Vermont movement of 2000. Targeting not only gays and lesbians but the state's changing demographics, the movement, though unsuccessful, infected the political campaigns of that year and dangerously inflamed passions. *My Mixed-Up Berry Blue Summer* does a lovely job of humanizing the more abstruse aspects of the politics involved and, in June, MJ, and Eva, offers fully realized characters with whom readers can empathize. **GA**

George, Madeleine
The Difference Between You and Me
Viking, 2012. 255 p. ISBN: 9780670011285

COULD THESE GIRLS BE ANY more different? Straight-arrow Emily is student council vice president; contrarian Jesse is founder (and sole member) of NOLAW (The National Organization to Liberate All Weirdos). Jesse is queer; Emily is (presumably) straight; so why are the two to be found each Tuesday afternoon making out in the public library's restroom? But wait, that's not all. Emily has secured both a student internship with and funding for the annual prom from North Star, corporate owner of StarMart, an uber retailer a la WalMart that is trying to secure community support for opening a new store. Needless to say, Jesse is outraged by this as is her new friend Esther. Together the two begin an anti-StarMart campaign that is almost sure to end badly (don't mess with The Man). Will Jesse's clandestine relationship with Emily also end badly? Stay tuned. George has written a plot-rich but fast-moving story of romance and social realism told from the alternating perspectives of all three girls. Not all the lessons they learn are happy ones but maybe, just maybe, if one is serious about fighting injustice and powerful vested interests, better times might be ahead. Power to the people! **GA, QC**

Going, K. L.
King of the Screwups
Harcourt, 2009. 310 p. ISBN: 9780547331669

SEVENTEEN-YEAR-OLD LIAM, who just can't seem to get a handle on his own life, is this novel's titular king. His situation dramatically worsens when his hard-driving CEO father walks into his home office to find Liam and a girl having drunken sex on

his executive desk. Yikes! Since slacker Liam has worn out his welcome at school too, the only solution seems to be to send him away while he gets his act together. But where? The unlikely answer is to live with his "Aunt" Pete, his father's gay brother, an all-night radio DJ and lead vocalist with Glitter, a glam-rock cover band that has been playing together since the 1970s. Liam and Pete haven't seen each other for ten years, since Pete arrived at his parents' housewarming party wearing a slinky red evening gown, high heels, and a wig. Now living with his uncle and going to a new school, Liam, "Mr. Popularity," tries to tone down his image and become a nerdy student but just can't stop being, well, Mr. Popularity. Finally it's up to gay Uncle Pete to help his straight nephew find himself. Going's take on Liam's problems is at once lighthearted and psychologically astute and the character of "Aunt" Pete is definitely a keeper. **GA, QC**

Gold, Rachel
Being Emily
Bella Books, 2012. 210 p. ISBN: 9781594932830

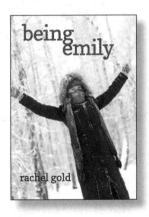

CHRISTOPHER HESSE LIVES WITH HIS mother, father, and nine-year-old brother, Mikey. He has a girlfriend, Claire, a place on the high school swim team, and a secret he can share with no one. Chris's physical body is male, but inside is a female named Emily. Chris lives in small-town Liberty, Minnesota, but his window into the larger world is GenderPeace, an online community for "people in the process of surviving transsexualism." The story, which follows Chris through his junior and senior years in high school, is told by Chris and Claire in alternating voices. Both are into Worlds of Warcraft, an online game world that is the only place Chris can be his true self in a female role—his favorite is Amalie, a powerful mage. In their companionable "going steady" mode, Claire has become Chris's closest friend and it is to her he first confides that, appearances to the contrary, he has been a girl all his life. *Being Emily* is purposive and didactic, but the information offered on transsexual and transgender people is accurate, and a story—even a rather didactic one—can effectively convey information in a manner that is a good fit for many teen readers. As Chris struggles to become Emily, he finds his father unexpectedly understanding, his mother unexpectedly harsh, his pesky little brother unexpectedly accepting, and his former girlfriend and current best friend, Claire, unexpectedly—and genuinely—empathetic. **HV**

Goldman, Steven

Two Parties, One Tux, and a Very Short Film about The Grapes of Wrath

Bloomsbury, 2008. 307 p. ISBN: 1599902710

SEVENTEEN-YEAR-OLD MITCHELL'S best friend, David, is gay, a fact that only Mitchell knows. Knowing this doesn't mean he understands it, however. "How," he wonders, "can this gay, non-cell-phone-carrying, pineapple-pizza-eating brown-bagger be so goddamned normal?" Normal or not, their relationship starts to change when David comes out: "I don't know how to act around you anymore," Mitchell uncomfortably admits. And things become even more uncomfortable when Mitchell discovers David has a crush on him. In the meantime Mitchell, who has a tiny problem with self-esteem, feels that he is "the single biggest loser on the face of the planet." So why does the hottest girl in his class suddenly become interested in him, even asking him to the prom? And what does all this have to do with a white tux and a very short film about *The Grapes of Wrath*? Goldman's first novel is an amusing, well-written coming-of-age story that includes a sensitive take on the ups and downs of adolescent friendship when one of the friends just happens to be gay. The result is an entertaining and sometimes thought-provoking read. **HV**

Goode, Laura

Sister Mischief

Candlewick Press, 2011. 367 p. ISBN: 9780763646400

HERE'S A COMING-OF-AGE NOVEL with a hip-hop beat. Esme and her friends Marcy, Tess, and Rohini have formed a white-girl hip-hop group they call Sister Mischief. When their high school administration banishes hip-hop from the school, the girls go subversive, forming an unsanctioned, queer-friendly (Esme is a lesbian) hip-hop student group they call 4H: Hip-Hop for Heteros and Homos. In the meantime Esme and Rohini have fallen in love and are maintaining a secret relationship because Rohini is terrified that her parents might learn of her homosexuality (or at least bisexuality; her sexual identity is still a work in progress). Can such a clandestine relationship endure? If it doesn't, what impact will it have on Sister Mischief? All of this culminates in a sneak-attack performance during a school assembly that will have a significant impact on the future of Sister Mischief, 4H, and the status of hip-hop music and culture at the school. Goode's first novel is a well-written and often amusing examination of hip-hop and student self-expression and a clear-eyed look at the occasional ambiguities of teenage sexuality. **GA, QC**

Green, John and David Levithan
Will Grayson, Will Grayson
Dutton, 2010. 320 p. ISBN: 9780525421580

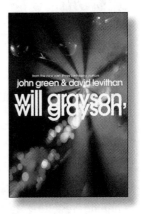

TWO OF YOUNG ADULT LITERATURE'S leading lights collaborate on this memorable LGBTQ novel. As the title indicates, there are two Will Graysons, one is straight, the other is gay. Initially they don't know each other though, before the novel ends, circumstances will bring them together. Here's the story (told in alternating chapters and voices): Straight Will's best friend is Tiny Cooper, "the world's largest person who is really, really gay and also the world's gayest person who is really, really large." A fabulous, take-charge kind of guy, Tiny has decided that Will, who is constitutionally opposed to caring, should hook up with Possibly Gay Jane (is she?). Meanwhile gay Will Grayson is busy being angry and depressed. The only good thing in his life is his online relationship with Isaac––whom he has, you guessed it, never met in person. When they finally arrange to meet, Isaac is a––surprise, surprise––a no show. And then fate––or something similar––brings gay Will and gayer Tiny together and things get interesting. In the meantime Tiny is busy trying to mount a production of his semiautobiographical musical "Tiny Dancer." Will straight Will and Possibly Gay Jane and gay Will and Tiny find true love? Will "Tiny Dancer" come to life onstage? Will *Will Grayson, Will Grayson* captivate its readers? Read this delightful and life-affirming novel for all the answers. **HV, GA**

Griffin, Molly Beth
Silhouette of a Sparrow
Milkweed, 2012. 208 p. ISBN: 9781571317018

THE YEAR IS 1926 AND sixteen-year-old Garnet has been sent to a resort hotel in Excelsior, Minnesota, to spend the summer with her stuffy, wealthy relatives. Determined to make her own way, she—to her relatives' disapproval—takes a part-time

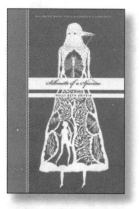

job in a milliner's shop. There she meets and quickly falls in love with beautiful flapper Isabella, who is a dancer in the local dance hall. The girls begin a secret relationship that is at once touching and tender. Meanwhile Garnet seeks to indulge her other great passion: birds. Her hope is to go to college and become a field biologist. But, given the circumstances of her family and the conventions of the times, this may be an impossible dream. Then again, it may be a possibility that Garnet can reach through her own efforts, determination, and hard work. The tone of the novel is old-fashioned—though perhaps not inconsistent with its period setting—and many of the characters are flat stock types, but happily, Garnet and Isabella are more fully realized, as is the setting. **HV**

Guran, Paula, ed.

Brave New Love:
15 Dystopian Tales of Desire

Running Press, 2012. 392 p. ISBN: 9780762442201

LOVE IS A SURVIVOR! Whether straight or gay, it has the power to endure the shudder-inducing likes of global warming, acid rain, pollution, and more in these fifteen darkly dystopian tales. As much fantasy as science fiction, few of these stories are set in *Blade Runner* dystopias. Instead they take place in post-industrial, agrarian societies and prove that love is not only brave and new but also as old as the human condition. Though familiar to speculative fiction fans, only three of the fifteen contributors will likely be familiar to general readers: William Sleator, Carrie Ryan, and Jeanne DuPrau. That said, all the contributions have universal appeal. **HV, GA**

Hacker, Randi

Life As I Knew It

Simon Pulse, 2006. 233 p. ISBN: 9781416909958

ANGELINA ROSSINI IS IN LOVE with Jax, who is gay. Several years later, this potential problem is but a momentary blip in their relationship as longtime best friends

and confidants. When Angelina's larger-than-life father, Andrea, suffers a stroke that leaves him mute and partially paralyzed, she is able to turn to Jax for comfort and also to her mother's best friend, Liz, who is a lesbian. Then Angelina discovers that her bête noire, Celeste, is a lesbian and actually has a crush on her. Yes, there is a great deal of gay content in this book that is, nevertheless, principally about how Angelina's life changes dramatically in the wake of her father's catastrophic illness. Jax remains the principal gay character in the book. While he is out to Angelina and his beloved grandmother, he is otherwise closeted, but though his rough-hewn family and many others in their small town suspect the truth there are no unpleasant repercussions. Indeed, Angelina and her friends are very accepting of the homosexuality of Jax, Liz, and Celeste. Is such acceptance idealistic or realistic? Does it matter? Well, not really, as their small town may be viewed as an ideal community in the manner of David Levithan's *Boy Meets Boy*. And that's a good thing. A very good thing. **GA**

Hand, Elizabeth
Radiant Days
Viking, 2012. 272 p. ISBN: 9780670011353

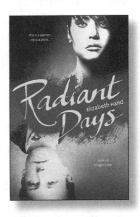

IT IS THE LATE 1970s in Washington, DC, and eighteen-year-old Merle, an artist from the Virginia hill country, is a student at the Corcoran School of Art. When the female instructor with whom she has been having an affair dumps her, Merle finds herself emotionally bereft and homeless. Having dropped out of art school, she becomes a graffiti artist, tagging her signature sunburst work "Radiant Days." The novel takes on an air of magical realism when, spending the night in a safe house, she meets sixteen-year-old French poet Arthur Rimbaud who has somehow time traveled from the year 1870. The two talented teens bond over art (both are gay, so there is no romantic attachment) and influence each other's work. The novel is told in alternating chapters from each teen's respective point of view, Merle's story being told in her first-person voice and Arthur's in the third person. Beautifully written, the book is a lyrical celebration of the power and glory of art. **GA**

Hardy, Mark

Nothing Pink

Namelos, 2008. 109 p. ISBN: 9781608981489

SECRETLY GAY, FOURTEEN-YEAR-OLD VINCENT, son of a Baptist minister, thinks, "I know if God doesn't save me, if I die before he rips the queer demons out by their roots, I'm going to burn in hell for all eternity." Yet pray though he might, Vincent senses that God seems unwilling or unable to change him. And then he meets Robert, a boy in his father's new congregation, and the two boys fall in love. Inevitably Vincent's parents discover his secret and, in a highly dramatic scene, pray over him, asking God to cast the "demons" out of their son. Despite this, Vincent knows nothing has changed vis-à-vis his orientation and, to his surprise, he begins to wonder if God might love him just as he is—certainly Robert does. Never melodramatic, Hardy's novel—the title refers to an outfit Vincent's mother dressed him in when he was a little boy—is a quiet, reflective look at the uneasy dialectic between homosexuality and fundamentalist religion. To his credit the author portrays the parents as loving but troubled by their son's homosexuality, while Vincent is at peace with himself and his love for Robert. Readers who enjoy this will want to read Alex Sanchez's *God Box*. **HV**

Harmon, Michael

The Last Exit to Normal

Knopf, 2008. 275 p. ISBN: 9780440239949

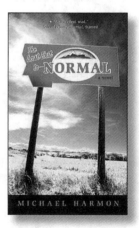

WHEN FOURTEEN-YEAR-OLD BEN'S father announces he's gay and his mother files for divorce, Ben—now living with his father—begins acting up, smoking pot and generally getting into trouble. Three years later the now seventeen-year-old has cleaned up his act, but when he is involved in a car crash following a high-speed police chase, enough is enough: Ben's father and his partner Edward respond by deciding (rather improbably) to leave Tacoma and its attendant temptations and move to Edward's small (population 400) hometown in eastern Montana. There they move in with Edward's mother, Mae, a harridan if ever there were one, who decides to civilize the spiky-haired, skateboard-riding Ben. While the boy shows progress, accelerated by his meeting and falling in love with a local girl, Kimberly, his relationship with his father remains fraught. Ben feels his father's actions in taking a male partner have been selfish and that he (Ben) has had to bear the brunt of the family's dislocation and the problems attendant upon it. Will the two be able to resolve their differences? And will they be able to fit into their conservative small town? An intriguing subplot involves a neighbor who batters his eleven-year-old son and Ben's sometimes misguided attempts to help the boy. Add this to the modest number of LGBT titles examining teens' dealing with a gay parent. **GA**

Harrington, Hannah
Speechless
Harlequin Teen, 2012. 288 p. ISBN: 9780373210527

LIKE MALINDA, PROTAGONIST OF Laurie Halse Anderson's much-lauded *Speak*, this novel features a female teen protagonist, Chelsea Knot, who tells the reader her story while remaining mute. Both protagonists are silent in response to trauma, but Chelsea's trauma—in this case, a homophobic hate crime—is one that her own careless words set in motion. Inveterate gossip Chelsea is on the popular crowd's A-list, best friend to queen bee Kristen. In the midst of a booze-filled, no-parents-home New Year's Eve party at Kristen's house, Chelsea is tipsily seeking a bathroom when she happens upon two boys from her school in a passionate embrace. And she can hardly *wait* to announce her juicy gossip to all the partygoers. Several boys—including Kristen's boyfriend—announce their gay-bashing intent, and the next morning Chelsea learns that one of the two boys she outed is hospitalized with critical injuries. Chelsea—clueless but not heartless—contacts the police and provides the information they need to arrest the attackers. Her painful regret at the harm her words have caused leads to her decision to take a vow of silence. Henceforth, she will communicate by written word only and carries a notepad with her for this purpose. Yes, the story is a didactic one, but having it told entirely from Chelsea's perspective makes her shift believable as she comes to understand that her words—for good of for ill— matter. **HV**

Harris, Michael
Homo
Lorimer, 2013. 142 p. ISBN: 9781459401914

WHEN WILL IS OUTED ON Facebook, he dreams of leaving Chilliwack, his tiny Canadian hometown, for a new life in Vancouver, as he has begun dating Riley, an older man he has met online. In the meantime life goes on as usual in Chilliwack.

Will hangs out with his longtime friend Julie and with Daniel, the only other out gay teen at Spencer High. While Will finds grudging acceptance, Daniel, who is flamboyantly gay, has a harder time of it, being subjected to taunts and to physical abuse until he is driven to do something desperate. There aren't many surprises in Harris's gay coming-of-age novel, and there are some stereotypical situations and characters, but Will, who is initially solipsistic and faux cynical, grows emotionally and, by the book's end, has matured and become significantly more likable than he was when the story began. His relationship with Riley is handled realistically, and its denouement is believable. A volume in Lorimer's Side Streets series, *Homo* is a quick and—aside from its unfortunate title—satisfying read. **GA**

Hartinger, Brent
Geography Club
(Volume 1 in the Russell Middlebrook series)
HarperCollins, 2003. 226 p.
ISBN: 9780060012236

RUSSEL MIDDLEBROOK IS A CLOSETED gay teen who is searching for kindred spirits: "I desperately wanted to be somewhere where I could be honest about who I was and what I wanted." He begins his search in an Internet chat room for gay youth, where he is astonished to learn that the friendly, nervous, and as-yet anonymous gay

teen he meets there is in fact Kevin, the handsome jock in his P.E. class. This discovery gives him the courage to come out to his best friend, Min, who responds with her own confession that she is having a romantic relationship with Terese, star of the girls' soccer team. These four, plus another gay friend, create a small safe space for themselves by becoming the Geography Club, an official after-school activity with a name they hope sounds sufficiently dull to discourage anyone else from joining. Thus, instead of looking elsewhere for a gay community, they set about successfully creating their own as they negotiate their school's social geography, which includes the Land of the Popular, the Borderlands of Respectability, and the dreaded Outcast Island. Russel's cleverly told account of the genesis and growth of the Geography Club is a story with humor and heart. **HV, QC**

Hartinger, Brent
The Order of the Poison Oak
Buddha Kitty Books, 2005. 180 p. ISBN: 9780984679447

VOLUME 2 in the Russell Middlebrook series. Russel and Min spend the summer at a camp for children who are recovering from severe burns. **GA**

Hartinger, Brent
Double Feature:
Attack of the Soul-Sucking Brain Zombies/ Bride of the Soul-Sucking Brain Zombies
Buddha Kitty Books, 2007. 276 p. ISBN: 9780984679430

VOLUME 3 in the Russell Middlebrook series. Two stories: Russel and Min each tell a story about their summer as extras in a horror movie. **GA.**

Hartinger, Brent
The Elephant of Surprise
Buddha Kitty Books, 2013. 226 p. ISBN: 9780984679454

VOLUME 4 in the Russell Middlebrook series, Russel falls for an anticonsumerist freegan who pops out of the school dumpster. **GA**

Hines, Sue
Out of the Shadows
AvonTempest, 2000. 213 p. ISBN: 9780380811922

SET IN AUSTRALIA, THIS IS the story of two girls, Rowanna and Jodie, and their best friend Mark. Though the story is told from the two girls' respective points of view, elfin and sometimes assertive Ro emerges as the main character. Her mother dead after being run down by a drunk driver, Ro lives with her mother's lover, Deb. Jodie is the beautiful new girl in school upon whom Mark has a crush. All three fifteen-year-olds have shadowy secrets. Jodie is a closeted lesbian, Mark is battered by his relapsed alcoholic father, and Ro feels she is responsible for her mother's

accidental death. Jodie comes out to Ro and Mark at Deb's suggestion but remains otherwise closeted. Mark's father, battering his son one time too many, finally understands that he must stop drinking and resumes attending AA meetings. It is Ro, however, who is battling the most persistent demons, attempting to put them to rest via journaling an account of her attempts to destroy her mother and Deb's relationship. It's not a pretty story, but it has the desired cathartic effect. Though occasionally a bit preachy, the novel boasts sympathetic characters and demonstrates to American readers the universality of the gay experience (see also books by Aidan Chambers and Eddie De Oliveira). **HV, QC**

Homes, A. M.
Jack
Macmillan, 1989. 240 p. ISBN: 9780679732211

FIFTEEN-YEAR-OLD JACK narrates this wryly humorous and realistic portrayal of the slow journey toward maturity as he learns to accept the things he cannot change, which range from his father's gayness to needing to take driver's education. Up to age eleven, Jack lived with his mother and father in a traditional nuclear family. Then one day Jack's father inexplicably moves out, leaving Jack with his aggrieved mother, unasked questions, and awkward silences. Jack's questions are finally answered when his father tells him that he is gay and in a committed relationship with his longtime roommate, Bob. Emotional mayhem ensues as Jack's father's gayness becomes fodder for school gossip. Jack is taunted as "fag baby," and readers will find his corrosive fury understandable but a bit tedious. There's more unavoidable discomfort for Jack in driver's education when a class session is devoted to viewing all-too-vivid videos of crushed cars, mutilated bodies, and weeping relatives. Part of him wants to run from the room, but another part hesitates: "if I ran I would flunk the class, I would never get my license, and I would never grow up . . . I stayed. I sat there, watched the movies, and felt sick." Jack's voice reflects the worrisome complexity of the life of a teen who simultaneously avoids and embraces his own transition from passenger to driver: "I was totally freaking out. I thought about how everyone always told me I could be whatever I wanted, that all I had to do was decide what it was and go after it. It was the go-after-it part I was just beginning to understand." **HV**

Hoole, Elissa Janine

Kiss the Morning Star

Marshall Cavendish, 2012. 240 p. ISBN: 9780761462699

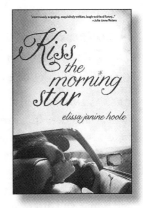

TOGETHER, SEVENTEEN-YEAR-OLD ANNA and her best friend Kat set off on a quixotic cross-country road trip with only Jack Kerouac's *Dharma Bums* as a guide. Each girl has her own reasons for embarking on the journey (which is, of course, symbolic): Anna is struggling to deal with her mother's death the previous year and her grief-stricken father's search for solace in alcohol abuse. Kat is trying to help her friend while also trying to search for evidence of God's love. Anna, whose father is a clergyman, has lost her faith but begins to find love in her increasingly intimate relationship with Kat. As the girls travel, their friendship deepens and turns into something richer and more complex. Hoole's first novel is a coming-of-age story that is enhanced by its success at creating multidimensional, empathetic characters for whom readers will care. It's an auspicious debut. **HV**

Hopkins, Ellen

Tilt

S&S/McElderry, 2012. 608 p. ISBN: 9781416983309

A YA COMPANION TO THE author's adult novel *Triangles*, this novel in free verse follows the unfortunate lives of three teens: Mikayla, Harley (who's a girl), and Shane. Though leading different lives, the three have in common difficulties with their dysfunctional families and problems with their romantic choices. Shane, who is gay, has fallen in love with a boy who is HIV positive. Unmarried Mikayla has become pregnant, and thirteen-year-old Harley has fallen for an older boy who is taking sexual advantage of her. Fans of Hopkins's gritty fiction will find much that is familiar here: a trio of teens whose lives range from the dysfunctional to the dire. Sometimes melodramatic, sometimes maudlin, the novel is redeemed for LGBTQ teens by Shane's story with its cautionary take on AIDS, a subject that is still vitally important but is rarely seen in recent YA fiction. **GA**

Horner, Emily

A Love Story Starring My Dead Best Friend

Dial, 2010. 259 p. ISBN: 9780803734203

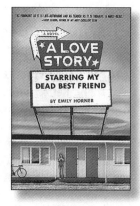

CASS IS IN LOVE WITH her straight best friend, Julia. When Julia dies in a car wreck, Cass decides to undertake a quixotic quest: as a tribute to her dead best friend, she will take the trip to California the two had planned—but on her bicycle carrying Julia's ashes. Will she make it? And what will she do when, returning home, she discovers that Heather, the girl who had called her a dyke and spread malicious rumors about her in middle school, is herself gay and has a crush on her? And will the two and their friends be able to mount a production of Julia's musical, *Totally Sweet Ninja Death Squad*, as a further tribute? If all of this sounds complicated, it is. Fortunately Horner is able to bring her story off without too much visible effort, though Cass's motivation is sometimes a bit shaky. That aside, *A Love Story* does a good job of managing its characters' emotions and of reminding readers that friendship is also a form of love. **GA**

Howe, James

The Misfits

Simon & Schuster, 2001. 274 p. ISBN: 9780689839566

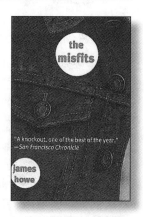

MEET THE FOUR MEMBERS OF the Gang of Five: Bobby the fat boy, Skeezie the hood, Joe the queer boy, and Addie the geek girl. As Bobby explains, "We call ourselves the Gang of Five, but there are only four of us. We do it to keep people on their toes. Make 'em wonder. Or maybe we do it because we figure that there's one more kid out there who's going to need a gang to be a part of. A misfit, like us." And *these* misfits are totally, *totally* fed up with their middle school's status quo of relentless name-calling and a student government that's been run by the same popular kids since forever. Their solution: form their own political party, the "No-Name Party," run for student council, and—they hope—shake up the establishment. Their wits are keen, their tongues are sharp, and their humor is relentless. The story is narrated by Bobby, whose account is interspersed with the often-hilarious minutes of the Gang of Five's weekly meetings at the Candy Kitchen, where they discuss important issues, eat ice cream, and plot to take over the world, starting with Paintbrush Falls Middle School. This book has inspired actual "no-name-calling" campaigns in schools across the United States. **GA, QC**

Howe, James
Totally Joe
Atheneum, 2005. 189 p. ISBN: 9780689839573

ANYONE WHO HAS READ HOWE'S novel *The Misfits* will know that Joe Bunch is not exactly your average Joe. This is a twelve-year-old boy who has owned seven Barbies, five rubber ducks, and an Easy-Bake Oven; who loves to dress up; who still has all his stuffed animals; who hates sports; and, oh yes, who has a terrific boyfriend named Colin. Yes, Joe is gay, but neither he nor Colin is out, so their relationship is strictly on the q.t. except among the Gang of Five: Joe's best friends, Bobby, Addie, and Skeezie (see *The Misfits*), who know everything about Joe—well, not *every* everything! But the reader does because Joe tells all in this alphabiography. What's an alphabiography? It's an autobiography built on the letters of the alphabet. Thus, A is for Addie. C is for Colin, of course. H is for Halloween, when Joe and Colin almost break up, and so on. The conceit is a clever one and well executed, while Joe's voice is witty (sometimes self-consciously so) and his story, though highly episodic, is totally engaging. *Totally Joe* is arguably the best of the handful of LGBTQ books aimed at middle school readers and is highly recommended. **HV, QC**

Hyde, Catherine Ryan
Becoming Chloe
Knopf, 2006. 215 p. ISBN: 9780375832604

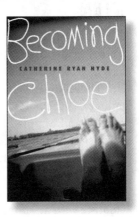

WHEN GAY TEENAGER JORDY RESCUES Chloe from a gang rape, the two bond and begin a life together on the street, with Jordy prostituting himself to help them survive. Chloe is childlike, innocent, even at times seeming to be simpleminded. But when her horrible past threatens to overwhelm her and perhaps drive her to suicide, Jordy decides they should take a cross-country road trip from Connecticut to California to demonstrate that the world is a beautiful, joyful place. In her first novel for teens, Hyde (*Pay It Forward*) has written a moving account of two teenagers' sometimes quixotic quest to find happiness. Jordy is perhaps the more sympathetic character, stalwart in his devotion to Chloe, whose fey persona occasionally tries the reader's patience. As for the homosexual content, it is intelligently and sympathetically handled. **GA**

Hyde, Catherine Ryan
Jumpstart the World
Knopf, 2010. 208 p. ISBN: 9780375866654

WHEN THE BOYFRIEND OF ELLE'S mother declares he doesn't like having teenagers around, the compliant mother rather improbably moves the fifteen-year-old girl into her own apartment. Once there, impressionable Elle meets and falls in love with Frank, the man next door. When her friends reveal to her that Frank is a female-to-male transgender person, she reacts with anger and incredulity, dumping the friends and then going into a state of deep denial about Frank. Though occasionally coming dangerously close to being a problem novel with, in stubborn Elle, a generally unsympathetic character, *Jumpstart the World* is redeemed by the wonderfully sympathetic character of Frank. In him, Hyde has written one of the best transgender characters in young adult literature. Readers who enjoy this fine novel will also want to read Julie Anne Peters's *Luna* and Cris Beam's *I Am J* and *Becoming Emily*. **HV, GA**

Jackson, Corrine
If I Lie
Simon Pulse, 2012. 288 p. ISBN: 9781442454132

QUINN IS A HIGH SCHOOL SENIOR living in Sweethaven, North Carolina, just west of Camp Lejeune. Nearly everyone there has some connection with the military. ("In our town there are three classes—poor, middle, and Marine.") This is Quinn's hometown, so when she and Carey, one of the boys she grew up with, start dating in high school, no one is surprised. Carey graduates early, enlists, and is deployed to Afghanistan; this too is business as usual. But after Carey leaves, a photo of Quinn in a romantic embrace with an unseen someone who is *not* Carey appears on Facebook. Cheating on a deployed soldier is viewed as near-treasonous in Sweethaven, and Quinn loses the respect of nearly everyone, including her father. When Carey disappears and is declared MIA, Quinn is shamed and shunned by all. However, before Carey left, Quinn became the first (and, thus far, only) person in town to know that Carey is gay. Their relationship is a friendship—nothing more—but it's Carey's secret, so Quinn swallows her anger at her undeserved pariah status, feeling honor bound to tell no one. In the midst of this, Quinn becomes involved in an oral history project at the local VA hospital, where she strikes up a friendship with a Vietnam vet, a stranger to Sweethaven, who sees her as a person, not as the town slut, and his outsider perspective makes a significant difference in her troubled life. **HV**

Jahn-Clough, Lisa
Country Girl, City Girl
Houghton Mifflin, 2004. 176 p. ISBN: 9780618447916

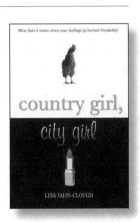

THIRTEEN-YEAR-OLD PHOEBE, whose mother died when she was two, lives on a farm in Maine with her father and brother. Hers is an isolated and sometimes lonely life until Melita, the fourteen-year-old daughter of her mother's high school best friend, comes from New York to spend the summer. Melita is vastly more sophisticated and self-confident than Phoebe, and when the two practice kissing, the country girl finds herself attracted to her city counterpart in ways that add up to more than simple friendship. When Phoebe subsequently visits Melita in the city, she discovers that her friend is attracted to a boy and feels betrayed. This modest coming-of-age novel with feminist overtones deserves notice as one of only a handful of LGBTQ novels aimed at middle school readers. **HV**

Jenkins, A. M.
Breaking Boxes
Delacorte Press, 1997. 182 p. ISBN: 9780385325134

TWO BROTHERS—SIXTEEN-YEAR-OLD CHARLIE and twenty-four-year old Trent, sons of a long-gone father and a mother who drank herself to death—are living on their own. Trent goes to college part-time and works in a bookstore to support himself and Charlie. Trent is gay, a fact that Charlie has known since he was "ten or eleven" and accepts completely. He is also aware that Trent keeps this part of his life "compartmentalized" to spare Charlie the perceived stigma of living with a gay person (even though that person is his brother, not his lover). Another kind of compartmentalization—class conflict—

is evidenced in Charlie's sometimes violent interactions with boys of privilege at his school. This begins to change, though, when Charlie befriends Brandon, one of the privileged. However, their growing friendship may be shattered if Brandon learns that Trent is gay. Jenkins's storytelling demonstrates an extraordinary ability to create multidimensional male characters, both straight and gay, and to capture the authentic sounds of their conversation. The revelation of a member's homosexuality ultimately strengthens the emotional viability of the family. **HV, GA**

Johnson, Alaya Dawn

The Summer Prince

Scholastic/Levine, 2013. 304 p. ISBN: 9780545417792

THIS WORK OF DYSTOPIAN FICTION is set in a post-nuclear-winter Brazil. There the survivors have built a matriarchal society housed in a towering pyramidal city of Palmares Tres, where every five years a prince is selected, chooses a queen, and after a year, is sacrificed. Class is stratified, the lowest classes being at the lowest level of the pyramid. It's from there that a beautiful young man named Enki is elected prince. A privileged seventeen-year-old artist named June (her mother is married to one of the governing Aunties) is drawn into Enki's world along with her best (male) friend, Gil. Both fall in love with Enki, who chooses Gil as his partner and June as an artistic collaborator. Together they make memorable art that creates a wave of discontent in Palmares Tres and then, as Enki's sacrifice draws nearer, attempt to escape, but what lies beyond the sheltered city? **GA**

Johnson, Maureen

On the Count of Three

Razorbill, 2004. 370 p. ISBN: 9781595141552

LIVING IN SARATOGA SPRINGS, New York, Nina, Mel, and Avery have been inseparable BFFs until the summer before their senior year, when Nina goes to a leadership camp at Stanford University, while Mel and Avery hold down summer jobs at P. J. Mortimer's Fine Food and Drinks Emporium, a faux-Irish strip-mall restaurant where the servers wear tweed caps, suspenders, and beer ad name tags (Shane O'Douls, Molly

Guinness). While at Stanford, Nina meets and falls for Steve, a West Coast environmentalist. When she returns home, she is dismayed to discover that in her absence Mel and Avery have become lovers, thus sundering the long-standing "Bermudez Triangle" (Bermudez is Nina's last name). The story then follows the girls and their new friend, Parker, throughout the course of their senior year as Nina's long-distance relationship begins to fray and Avery begins to question her attraction to Mel. A bereft Mel comes out to her family and turns to Nina for comfort and understanding. All three girls are vividly portrayed, as is the strength of their friendship, the discomfort that a trio of BFFs face when the relationship between two of them becomes sexual and the ways in which serious life issues and humor intertwine. A work of commercial fiction, this romantic coming-of-age novel is notable for being one of the first LGBTQ YA novels to be targeted at the retail (instead of the traditional institutional) market. **HV, QC**

Juby, Susan
Another Kind of Cowboy
HarperTeen, 2007. 344 p. ISBN: 9780060765187

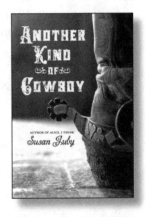

WHEN HIS FATHER WINS a horse in a card game, sixteen-year-old Alex becomes a champion Western rider, a real cowboy, much to his father's delight. However, the boy's heart belongs to dressage. Secretly taking lessons in the elegant sport, he meets Cleo, a girl from California who has come to Canada (the book is set on Vancouver Island) to attend a combination boarding and riding school and who winds up taking lessons from Alex's riding teachers, a retired gay couple. As it happens, Alex is also gay, though not openly so. He and Cleo, whose family is exceptionally rich, gradually become friends. Alex finds his heart set on Chris, his straight best friend, even though, as he thinks, "For a gay guy to get a crush on his straight friend was practically suicidal." But is Chris straight? Hmmm. In the meantime Alex has another problem: coming out to his father as both secretly gay *and* a dressage student! Yikes! Juby has written a delightfully funny and heartfelt story of a boy trying to break out of his compartmentalized life and find the freedom to be who he is. The riding aspect of the story is interesting and may make dressage fans of its readers, who will already be fans of Alex and Cleo. **HV, GA**

Katcher, Brian

Almost Perfect

Delacorte Press, 2009. 368 p. ISBN: 9780385906203

TRYING TO RECOVER FROM THE end of his relationship with Brenda, eighteen-year-old Logan notices a new girl at his small hometown high school, a tall and undeniably cute redhead named Sage. He is immediately attracted to her, and it appears the feeling is mutual. As he gets to know Sage better, he learns that she is forbidden to date until she graduates from high school. But why? And why has she been homeschooled for the four preceding years? When the two finally kiss, Sage reveals that she is male-to-female transgender. Horrified that anyone finding out Sage's secret will assume he is homosexual, Logan breaks off their relationship. A distraught Sage then attempts suicide, and Logan begins to rethink his rejection of her. Katcher has written a sensitive, emotionally engaging novel about a transgender teen attempting to deal with the problems—including an emotionally abusive father—surrounding her transition. Fans of this novel will want to read Rachel Gold's *Being Emily* and Ellen Wittlinger's *Parrotfish*. **HV**

Kerr, M. E.

Deliver Us from Evie

HarperCollins, 1994. 179 p. ISBN: 9780060244750

SIXTEEN-YEAR-OLD MISSOURI FARM BOY Parr Burman tells the story of his older sister, eighteen-year-old Evie, who looks like a young Elvis Presley, enjoys repairing farm machinery, and is jeeringly called Parr's "brother" by the other boys at school. Yes, Evie is a lesbian and she looks the part. "Some of us look it, Mom!" Evie tells her mother. "I know you so-called normal people would like it better if we looked as much like all of you as possible, but some of us don't, can't, and never will!" Things take a dramatic turn when Evie falls in love with the beautiful Patsy Duff, daughter of the local banker. When Parr inadvertently outs Evie and Patsy to their entire rural community the two young women flee to St. Louis, then to Paris and finally settle in New York. But where do they now stand with their families? Can they go home again? Do they want to? Edwards Award-winner Kerr plays with stereotypes in this, one of her best novels. As she wrote of gays and lesbians in her Foreword to Roger Sutton's 1994 book *Hearing Us Out: Voices from the Gay and Lesbian Community*, "It took a while to grasp the meaning of gay pride and that it did not mean looking and acting as straight as possible." *Deliver Us from Evie* remains one of the best LGBTQ novels of the nineties and is inarguably one of the very best lesbian novels in the literature. It's a must read. **HV, GA, QC**

Kerr, M. E.
"Hello," I Lied
HarperCollins, 1997. 171 p. ISBN: 9780064471930

LANG PENNER, SEVENTEEN, IS GAY and in a relationship with Alex, who is several years older and is pressing the boy to come out. Meanwhile, Lang and his mother are spending the summer at Roundelay, a retired rock star's Long Island, New York, estate, where his mother has been hired as cook. When Alex accepts a welcome opportunity to act in a high-profile summer-stock company near Boston, Lang is both frustrated and relieved: his commitment to Alex is genuine, but his discomfort at being seen as part of a gay couple is equally genuine. The rock star's niece Huguette, an attractive gamine from rural France, arrives to spend the summer with her uncle (and be kept away from her boyfriend, an "unsuitable" young farmer). The uncle knows Lang is gay and therefore a suitably safe male escort for his niece. At first reluctant, Lang finds himself powerfully drawn to Huguette's fresh beauty, lively physicality, and genuine interest in him. The reader may not find Huguette all that charming, but Lang's attraction is believable. The first YA novel to explore bisexuality. **HV**

Kerr, M. E.
Night Kites
Harper & Row, 1986. 216 p. ISBN: 9780064470353

KERR IS ONE OF YOUNG adult literature's courageous groundbreakers, as witness this novel, the first about the previously taboo subject of AIDS. Published five years after the first appearance of the deadly disease, the novel remained controversial for some years. In her memorable acceptance speech for the Margaret A. Edwards Award for lifetime achievement in young adult literature, Kerr noted that this was one of her many books that she was often asked by administrators not to speak about when she was making school visits. Told by seventeen-year-old Erick Rudd, the story is about his twenty-seven-year-old brother Pete, a teacher and science fiction writer living in New York, who contracts AIDS, comes out to his devastated family and then returns home for his final illness. To his credit, Erick accepts his brother's homosexuality with refreshing equanimity, telling his father, "It's just another way of being. It's not a crime; it's not anything to be ashamed of." The father is less than sanguine, insisting that Pete's sexuality and illness remain a closely guarded secret. But is that possible as Pete's illness worsens? Erick doesn't blame Pete, and the illness that might have driven them apart instead brings the brothers closer together. The publication of this pioneering book ushered in a modest body of AIDS literature for teen readers that appeared throughout the rest of the eighties and the early nineties. Kerr's remains inarguably the finest of the lot. **HV**

King, A. S.

Ask the Passengers

Little, Brown, 2012. 296 p. ISBN: 9780316194686

SEVENTEEN-YEAR-OLD ASTRID likes to lie on the family picnic table in the backyard and send love to the passengers in the planes she sees flying overhead. As she sees it, giving her love means that no one can control it. "If I give it all away," she thinks, "I'll be free." Astrid feels constricted by the conventions of her small town and hates the gossip that is epidemic there because she has secrets. "I have different secrets hidden from different people in different areas of my life," she thinks ruefully. Her best friend, Katrina, for example, is secretly gay, as is Justin, Katrina's "boyfriend." And no one—not even Katrina—knows that Astrid loves her new friend Dee. Does this mean Astrid is gay too? Well, it's complicated because what she hates most in the whole world is the idea of being put into a box or a category or a cage: "I'm not in this to be a member of some club," she thinks. But nevertheless, she loves Dee and Dee loves her. Things get truly complicated when Astrid and her friends go dancing at a gay club. The club is raided, after which they are held by the police for being underage, and now *everyone* knows their secrets. How will this affect Astrid's relationship with Dee? No spoilers here, but it is safe to say that airplane passengers can no longer have all of Astrid's love because, she thinks, "I have too many uses for it now." King's thoughtful and subtle novel belongs on the short list of the very best LGBT YA novels of the past several decades. **HV**

Klise, James

Love Drugged

Flux, 2010. 312 p. ISBN: 9780738721750

WHAT IF THERE WERE A drug that could "cure" homosexuality? When closeted gay teen Jamie decides to start dating a girl to further conceal his sexual orientation, he discovers that her scientist father is working on just such a drug. Uneasy with his sexual identity and terrified others will learn he is gay, the fifteen-year-old boy begins stealing samples of the untested drug. In the meantime, in a parallel story, his best friend, Wesley, who is hyperactive, decides to take himself off Ritalin. Both actions have unexpected consequences. Though the well-paced science fiction story (something of a rarity in LGBT fiction) combines humor with suspense, it also addresses serious ethical issues of medical technology's ability to alter identities. A good read that also offers excellent opportunities for discussion. **HV**

Kluger, Steve

My Most Excellent Year

A Novel of Love, Mary Poppins, and Fenway Park

Dial, 2008. 403 p. ISBN: 9780803732278

IT'S A MOST EXCELLENT YEAR! Augie realizes he's gay and falls in love with Andy. Not to be outdone, his lifelong best friend and passionate baseball fan, T.C., falls in love with Alejandra. She, in turn, falls in love with him *and* with acting. And together the teens help a lovable six-year-old deaf boy named Hucky realize his dream of meeting Mary Poppins. Bright, funny, and warmhearted, Kluger's novel is easily the feel-good book of the year. Its treatment of homosexuality is sensitive, sympathetic, and spot-on. In its spirit and tone it may remind some readers of David Levithan's *Boy Meets Boy* (q.v.). Augie's sexual preference is simply an accepted part of who he is, and his comfort with his sexual identity even inspires two other boys to come out. There is a hiccup in his relationship with Andy when the latter suggests Augie should dial down his flamboyance, but their falling out of love lasts about fifteen minutes before they're happily back together. Told in multiple voices and in some nontraditional narrative forms (school assignments, e-mails, texts, etc.), the book offers well-rounded characters and a lively, innovative plot. Highly recommended. **GA**

Knowles, Jo
See You at Harry's
Candlewick Press, 2012. 310 p. ISBN: 9780763654078

TWELVE-YEAR-OLD FERN wonders if all families are as frustrating to live with as hers. She's the third of four children, but the only one who ever seems to notice her is her three-year-old brother, Charlie. But then, other family members are, well, occupied. Her dad is busy promoting Harry's, the family restaurant; he mother is busy meditating; her older sister, Sarah, who is taking a gap year off from school, is busy trying *not* to work at Harry's; and her older brother, Holden, is trying to deal with being gay and to survive his daily ordeal on the school bus. But then he finds a friend, a senior in the high school where Holden is only a freshman. If this sounds like a fairly typical family story (though an extremely well-done one), it is, until something unthinkable happens and the story takes a dark turn. And Fern feels responsible. A fatal accident comes without any foreshadowing and divides the book into two disparate halves that don't quite work together, but Knowles's handling of the subplot involving Holden is spot-on and, for LGBTQ readers and their allies, redeems the book's shortcomings. **GA**

Koertge, Ron
Boy Girl Boy
Harcourt, 2005. 176 p. ISBN: 9780152058654

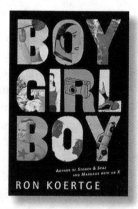

HIGH SCHOOL GRADUATION IS APPROACHING and BFFs Elliot, Teresa, and Larry have decided to skip college and get out of town; the day after graduation they're heading for California, far from their small and narrow-minded Illinois hometown. But wait. As the teens plan their trip, they start to rethink its viability. Readers hear the story in the voices and from the perspectives in rotation, giving them an opportunity to get to know each character in turn: their pasts, current lives, and hopes for the future. Elliott is a good-looking and athletic golden boy, but while his father dreams of his son's playing Big Ten football, the boy struggles academically—*his* dreams definitely don't include college. Teresa is an ardent runner who may be literally running away from her life's problems: abandoned by her mother at thirteen, she's developed an eating disorder and harbors an unrequited crush on Elliott. Larry is gay, a devoted film buff who loves watching movies but must deal with the bullying of local homophobes. A near tragedy invites the teens to reevaluate their lives, their futures, and their interrelationships. Koertge has written another character-driven novel that is both witty and wise, and Larry is a standout with whom readers of all orientations will empathize. **GA**

Koertge, Ron
The Arizona Kid
Joy Street, Little Brown, 1988. 228 p.
(Candlewick Press, 2005: ISBN: 9780763626952)

SIXTEEN-YEAR-OLD BILLY heads to Tucson, Arizona, to spend the summer with his gay uncle, Wes, whom he's never met. Billy, who is straight and lives in a small town in the Midwest, has reservations about living with "somebody who was really different from me. Somebody who was homosexual." Happily, Uncle Wes is anything but a stereotypical gay man (though he is a neat freak and, Billy thinks, "the best-looking guy I'd ever seen outside of the movies"). Compassionate and principled, he is a prominent local citizen and an AIDS activist. Though Tucson is hardly Bradleyville, Missouri—Billy's hometown—it is not without its share of homophobia, which touches Billy and Uncle Wes's lives. As noted, AIDS is a presence in the book, and one of Uncle Wes's friends dies of the disease. When Wes and his fellow activists hold a public healing service, he is threatened and pursued by a group of potential gay bashers, but he takes this with admirable equanimity: "Another opening, another show," he calmly tells Billy as he shuts and locks the front door. Koertge's novel is notable for its salutary use of humor and for the fact that Uncle Wes is sexually active (though he carefully practices safe sex), the first time an adult is so depicted in YA LGBTQ literature. *The Arizona Kid* is, hands down, one of the very best LGBT books of the 1980s and remains on the short list of the best LGBT books ever. It's a must read. **HV, GA, QC**

Kokie, E. M.
Personal Effects
Candlewick Press, 2012. 352 p. ISBN: 9780763669362

DEVASTATED AND ENRAGED BY THE violent death of his soldier brother, T. J., in Iraq, seventeen-year-old Matt begins acting out at school, his grades suffer, and he is suspended after he assaults a fellow student who is a pacifist and critical of

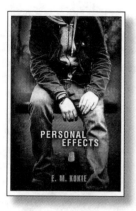

the war in Iraq. If his school life is bleak, his home life is even worse, made intolerable by the constant bullying of his ex-military father, who insists that Matt enlist. Going through T. J.'s personal effects, Matt discovers sometimes passionate love letters from a woman named Celia and evidence that his brother might have fathered a child with her. Hoping to find closure, Matt drives from his Pennsylvania home to Madison, Wisconsin, where Celia lives. Once there he finds not closure but the truth about his brother's secret life. How will he deal with this shocking truth, and what will it mean for his future? Told in Matt's first-person, present-tense voice, Kokie's debut novel is an intense, emotionally involving study of loss, grief, and resolution. **HV**

Konigsberg, Bill
Openly Straight
Scholastic/Levine, 2013. 320 p. ISBN: 9780545509893

NOW A JUNIOR IN HIGH SCHOOL, Rafe, who has been out since he was fourteen, is thoroughly sick of being labeled "the gay kid." So he does something bold: he leaves his Colorado high school to enroll in a private boys' school in New England, where no one knows he's gay, where he can be label free, no longer different, "openly straight," and just part of a group of guys. Does this mean he goes back into the closet? No, he tells himself, not exactly: "It was more like I was in the doorway . . . ." But is he fooling himself? Can you put a major part of yourself on hold, and what happens when you then find yourself falling in love with your new (straight) best friend? Lambda Literary Award–winner Konigsberg (*Out of the Pocket*) has written an exceptionally intelligent, thought-provoking coming-of-age novel about the labels that people apply to us and that we, perversely, apply to ourselves. Though a sometimes painful story of self-discovery, it is also a beautifully written, utterly captivating love story of two boys, Rafe and Ben, who are wonderfully sympathetic characters. With its capacity to invite both thought and deeply felt emotion, *Openly Straight* is altogether one of the best gay novels of the last ten years. **HV, GA**

Konigsberg, Bill
Out of the Pocket
Dutton, 2008. 264 p. ISBN: 9780525479963

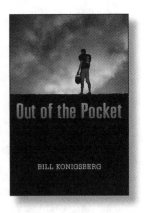

BOBBY FRAMINGHAM IS THE STAR quarterback of his California high school football team, and he has a secret: he's gay. When a reporter for their high school newspaper betrays Bobby's trust and outs him, it becomes national news. For as one reporter notes, "not one single openly gay man has ever actively competed in one of the four major American sports." Could Bobby, also an anomaly in high school sports, possibly become the first to do so professionally someday? In the meantime, however, he must deal with the fallout from being outed. Happily his teammates are, for the most part, sympathetic as are the other students at his high school. The media, of course, are all over him and Bobby must decide if he wants to hide or shun them. Or will he instead answer their questions as honestly as he can? And if he does, what will it mean to his life and future? Konigsberg, himself a sportswriter, has written an important book, one that not only addresses the ethics of outing a gay person but also fills a gap in GLBT literature: a sports story—and a good one, at that. Highly recommended. **HV**

Korman, Gordon
Born to Rock
Hyperion, 2006. 261 p. ISBN: 9780786809219

WHEN LEO ATTEMPTS TO HELP his friend Owen on a test, he is falsely accused of cheating and loses his scholarship to Harvard. End of the world, right? Well, maybe not. It appears that Leo may be the biological son of legendary punk rocker Marion X. McMurphy, aka King Maggot, lead singer for the band Purge. Hoping to persuade the man to loan him the money for his tuition, Leo signs on as a roadie for Purge's national tour. Tagging along as groupies are Owen, who turns out to be gay, and Melinda, Leo's lifelong friend. Korman does a good job of creating the chaotic world of a touring band and developing Leo's relationships with King, Owen, and Melinda. Though Owen is at first only a minor character who happens to be gay, he comes into his own as the plot begins to percolate and becomes something of a hero as Leo's plans begin to unravel. Though not as funny as some of Korman's other romps, *Born to Rock* has its moments of hilarity and, all in all, is a genial reading experience. **GA**

LaRochelle, David
Absolutely, Positively Not
Scholastic/Levine, 2005. 219 p. ISBN: 9780439591096

SIXTEEN-YEAR-OLD STEVEN goes square dancing each week . . . with his mother! And he enjoys it!! Does that mean he's (gasp) gay? Absolutely, positively not! Well . . . he *does* notice that when Coach Bowman smiles, his sky blue eyes smile as well, making it difficult to concentrate on anything else. Does that make him gay? Absolutely, positively not! After all, doesn't he have pictures of scantily clad women plastered on his school notebooks and bedroom walls? Doesn't he go out on twenty-three dates with twenty-one girls? "What other guy at school could claim such an impressive record?" he crows. But none of this does any good; he's still dreaming about boys. And so it is that he finally says those two little words to his best friend Rachel: "I'm gay." Yes, absolutely, positively gay! But of course, he swears her to secrecy, which is why he winds up taking a golden retriever to the prom (don't ask!). Other antic misadventures follow, each zanier than the one before until he can finally say, affirmatively, "I was feeling absolutely, positively gay." Steven is a great kid, and LaRochelle's first novel is an absolute delight, one of the very few humorous coming-out stories, and one that has an unabashedly happy ending. Highly recommended. **HV**

Larson, Rodger
What I Know Now
Henry Holt, 1997. 262 p. ISBN: 9780805048698

SET IN 1957 IN RURAL Stockton, California, this memoir-like novel is the story of Dave Ryan's fourteenth summer. His mother has inherited her family home, which enables her to leave her brutal husband, taking Dave with her. The two move in and begin to restore the abandoned house, and his mother hires a master gardener to restore the grounds. "Gene Tole came to the Home Place to build a garden for my mother and I fell in love with him, but didn't know it at the time," he later reflects. Throughout the summer Dave works alongside Gene and learns that a man can appreciate beauty, cook a meal, talk about ideas. This is, after all, the 1950s, and Gene is apparently closeted, but it is clear to the reader that the world is beginning to change, and Dave is changing as well. "By the end of the summer I wasn't the same any more." Gene provides Dave with glimpses of the larger world outside Stockton—even introducing him to the then-novel Italian specialty, pizza!—and in doing so, helps Dave begin to imagine his own future. **HV, QC**

Lecesne, James
Trevor
Seven Stories Press, 2012. 111 p. ISBN: 9781609804201

THIRTEEN-YEAR-OLD TREVOR is a sunny, upbeat teen with a quirky sense of humor . . . until the other kids at school decide he's gay and begin bullying him. The boy he has idolized turns against him, and the last straw comes when he arrives at school to discover somebody has scratched the word "faggot" on his locker. Trevor decides to commit suicide. Fortunately the strategy he employs—taking an overdose of aspirin—fails. "The people at the hospital informed me that a person cannot commit suicide by taking too many aspirin," he observes. "But they pretty much guaranteed me that I wouldn't have a headache for like another year." Will he try again? Perhaps, but in the meantime he decides to follow the advice of a young male hospital candy striper to take life one day at a time. This engaging—but slight—novella tells the story that inspired its author, Lecesne, to found the Trevor Project, the only nationwide twenty-four-hour crisis intervention and suicide prevention lifeline for lesbian, gay, transgender, and questioning teens. The story also inspired the creation of an eighteen-minute Academy Award–winning film. *Trevor* is a quick but important read. **HV**

Levithan, David
Boy Meets Boy
Knopf, 2003. 208 p. ISBN: 9780375832994

PAUL, FIFTEEN, NARRATES THE STORY of his ordinary teen life, telling of friends, tunes, family, afterschool activities, and dreams in his anything-but-ordinary hometown. "There isn't really a gay scene or a straight scene in our town," he notes.

"They got all mixed up a while back, which I think is for the best." The quirky bits of Paul's experience are delightful (the I Scream Parlor, where teens can drink malts while watching horror movies) and even subversive (the school team's star quarterback, the self-named Infinite Darlene, is elected homecoming queen), but all the elements are clever, goofy, sort of Edenic, and sort of fairy-tale-come-true. The story opens on an ordinary Friday evening. Paul and his friends are hanging out at a local chain bookstore, where they are grooving to live music and checking out the scene. And then . . . (cue "Some Enchanted Evening") Paul spots Noah—green eyes, tousled hair, cool sneakers—who just might be the guy of Paul's dreams. Suddenly shy, Paul at first hesitates but then introduces himself. "I can flirt with the best of them," he says, "but only when it doesn't matter. This suddenly matters." The two embark on a romantic boy-meets-boy journey as they meet, grow closer, encounter obstacles, overcome obstacles—all the elements of an ordinary romance presented in an extraordinary manner that feels like wish fulfillment at its finest. Enjoy your visit! **GA, QC**

Levithan, David

How They Met and Other Stories

Knopf, 2008. 244 p. ISBN: 9780375948862

IN AN AUTHOR'S NOTE Levithan states that these are stories about love, not love stories. "'Love stories' has the wrong feel to it," he explains. While many readers might think this is a subtle distinction, there is no gainsaying the fact that the eighteen stories in this fine collection are headquartered in the heart, not the head. Eight of these stories have LGBTQ content. What are they about? One is told by a boy who develops a serious crush on the cute counter boy at Starbucks ("Now it has to be one of Starbucks's more brilliant marketing strategies to maintain at least one completely dreamy guy behind the counter at any given shift"); another is about a boy who discovers his homosexuality in the backseat of a prom-bound limo; one is narrated by a girl who falls in love with, yes, the new girl in class ("The minute I saw Ashley, I thought, 'Oh, shit. Trouble'"); still another is about a boy who is interviewed for college admission by his boyfriend's father, while said boyfriend is listening at the door. And so it goes. While the content varies and there are no obvious connections among them, the stories share a substance and attitude that is winsome, wistful, witty, and wise. That one of the collection's stories was written when Levithan was still in high school evidences the fact that this is a younger writer who is a Wunderkind, and YA literature is the richer for it. **HV, GA**

Levithan, David
Love Is the Higher Law
Knopf, 2009. 167 p. ISBN: 9780375834684

LEVITHAN'S HAUNTING AND AFFECTING 9/11 novel examines the cataclysmic event through the intersecting lives of three New York teens: Clare, Peter, and Jasper. The three young people experience the immediate event differently: Claire, in school; Peter, in line at Tower Records; and Jasper, asleep in bed after a late, alcohol-infused night. Claire and Peter are classmates. Jasper is older, a college student, who has met Peter at a party and is supposed to meet him again for a date. In time the two will come together and begin a sweet-spirited relationship as all three find ways to cope with the devastating sense of grief and loss fostered by the attack on the twin towers. A New Yorker himself, Levithan brings a highly personal sensibility to this difficult material that will help readers emotionally engage with a historic event that they may be too young to have experienced personally. An important book for both individual reading and classroom use. **GA**

Levithan, David
The Realm of Possibility
Knopf, 2004. 210 p. ISBN: 9780375836572

"HERE'S WHAT I KNOW ABOUT the realm of possibility—it is always expanding, it is never what you think it is." So writes Levithan in his second novel, and his first novel in verse. The form is a perfect fit for his narrative strategy: to give twenty disparate teenagers their own voices to tell their varied but interconnected stories. A number of them feature LGBTQ content; for example, the story of the girl who writes love songs for a girl she can't have; the boys who share a forbidden pack of cigarettes that cements their relationship; the story of two boys whose love should be impossible but who are, nevertheless, celebrating their first anniversary ("Forgetting our gender / ignoring all the strange roads that led to us / being in the same time and place, there is still / the simple impossibility of love . . . but instead, I love him.") In *The Realm of Possibility* Levithan demonstrates his poetic capacity for language and for limning the features of love. His teenagers bring their cares and concerns, their lives and loves alive in his free verse lines. Here is another of Levithan's memorable contributions to the realm of LGBTQ literature. **HV, GA**

Levithan, David
Two Boys Kissing
Knopf, 2013. 208 p. ISBN: 9780307931900

LEVITHAN'S AFFECTING NOVEL is the story of two ex boyfriends, Harry and Craig, who hope to break the Guiness Book of World Record's longest sustained kiss, which clocked in at thirty-two hours, twelve minutes, and nine seconds. They kiss not only to break a record but to protest a hate crime that has been visited on a friend. Meanwhile, another couple, Peter and Neil, are having difficulties with their relationship. Also figuring in the story are Avery, a pink-haired transgender character, his boyfriend Ryan, and Cooper, who is single and addicted to online sex sites. The novel is narrated by "us," a kind of Greek chorus of gay men from the 1980s, a decade marked by the AIDS epidemic and ancillary political activism. The narrative device works to beautiful, haunting effect. The result is another one of Levithan's singular contributions to the body of LGBTQ literature. **HV, GA, QC**

Levithan, David
Wide Awake
Knopf, 2006. 221 p. ISBN: 9780375834677

IT IS THE NOT-TOO-DISTANT FUTURE and something unprecedented has occurred: Abraham Stein is elected the first openly gay and Jewish president of the United States. Or is he? The governor of the state of Kansas, which Stein carried by a scant 1,000 votes, has demanded a recount, one that has all the hallmarks of being fixed against Stein. In response some two million Americans—some for Stein, some against—have descended upon Kansas. Among them are Duncan and his boyfriend Jimmy. Just as there is uncertainty around the election, so there is uncertainty about the future of the two boys' relationship. Similar problems are visiting the relationship between their friends Keisha and Mira. Will Stein's election survive the call for a recount? Will the relationship of Duncan and Jimmy, of Keisha and Mira survive? These uncertainties add drama to this serious and heartfelt examination of an America torn by a historic election. Though occasionally—and perhaps unavoidably—didactic, the smoothly written story remains a compelling and thought-provoking one and demonstrates, yet again, that Levithan is arguably the finest author writing LGBTQ YA fiction today. **GA**

Lieberman, Leanne
Gravity
Orca, 2008. 245 p. ISBN: 9781554690497

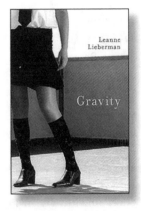

RELIGION IS SURPRISINGLY LITTLE represented in LGBT fiction, so this novel is a welcome exception. It's the story—told in her own first person voice—of fifteen-year-old Ellie Gold who, coming from an Orthodox Jewish family, is struggling with her sexuality. While spending the summer with her religiously liberal grandmother she meets and falls in love with the girl next door, Lindsay. The two begin a relationship that, if discovered, would be anathema to the religiously observant, leaving Ellie with a difficult choice: maintain her relationship or abandon her community. Which will she choose? The Canadian setting is well realized as are the characters who inhabit Ellie's life. Other LGBTQ novels with religious content include *My Father's Scar* by Michael Cart, *Nothing Pink* by Mark Hardy, and *The God Box* by Alex Sanchez. **HV**

Lo, Malinda
Adaptation
Little, Brown, 2012. 386 p. ISBN: 9780316197960

IT STARTS WITH A SERIES of plane crashes brought on by midair collisions with flocks of birds. It continues when, fleeing an ensuing riot, Reese and her debate partner, David, are seriously injured in an automobile accident and wake up twenty-seven days later in a top-secret advanced medical facility somewhere in Nevada (could it be the notorious Area 51, which is suffused by alien conspiracy theories?). Sworn to secrecy about their treatment, Reese and David, on whom she has had a long-time crush, return home to other anomalies, including the impossibly rapid healing of their injuries. Reese also has hallucinations and strange dreams that might be related to what happened while she was in a coma. Then she meets beautiful Amber and discovers her heart has had secrets of its own. "See," Amber says, "I told you, you're not straight." From this point the plot fluctuates between romance and science fiction adventure, not always to good effect because the romance, at least initially, tends to slow the action. Nevertheless, *Adaptation* is a fascinating, *X-Files*-type adventure that holds readers' attention to its inconclusive ending, which promises a sequel. **HV, GA**

Lo, Malinda

Ash

Little, Brown, 2009. 264 p. ISBN: 9780316040099

ASH, MALINDA LO'S FIRST NOVEL, is a dreamlike yet solid retelling of Cinderella with a strong thread of women loving women woven throughout. Aisling, called Ash, lives with her parents at the edge of a vast forest. Some say elves and fairies live in the forest; others say this is mere superstition, but still, villagers hesitate to open their doors at night for fear of what they may unwittingly invite into their homes. Aspects of British and Celtic folklore—the Wild Hunt, changelings, and fairy rings—give the story a European Middle Ages flavor. Ash's mother suddenly dies, and Ash is bereft. A short while later her merchant father sets off on a trading journey and returns with an unpleasant new wife and her two equally unpleasant daughters. When Ash's father dies a short time later, nearly penniless, Ash becomes the household's sole servant. But here the story diverges from its source with the introduction of two intriguing characters: Sidhean, a beautiful elven man with white hair and jewel-like blue eyes, and Kaisa, the king's charismatic huntress. When the king decides that his son must have a bride, the Cinderella story is set in motion, but Ash's story is her own. **HV**

Lo, Malinda

Huntress

Little, Brown, 2011. 371 p. ISBN: 9780316039994

WHEN THE FAIRY QUEEN INVITES King Cai Simin Tan to visit her kingdom, Taisin and Kaede, two seventeen-year-old girls who are fellow students at the Academy, are chosen to make the perilous journey with the king's son, Con. Soon the two girls

realize that they love each other, but Taisin is destined to become a sage, which means taking a vow of celibacy. Will the two be able to forge a lasting relationship? And indeed, will they survive their dangerous journey? This prequel to Lo's celebrated novel *Ash* is a richly imagined and plotted fantasy filled with dark magic and feats of derring-do exciting enough to satisfy the most demanding of readers. The tender relationship that develops between the two girls is realistic and emotionally satisfying. LGBT content is fairly rare in fantasy, making this a significant title and, happily, a compelling read. **HV**

Lockhart, E.

Dramarama

Hyperion, 2007. 311 p. ISBN: 9780786838172

BEST FRIENDS AND MUSICAL THEATER buffs Sarah and Demi are thrilled when they are both accepted as students at a six-week summer theater camp away from their stultifyingly small Ohio hometown. Demi, who is gay and has purposely kept a low profile, quickly comes into his own, demonstrating abundant talent and quickly landing two leading roles in camp productions—plus a boyfriend! The highly opinionated Sarah,

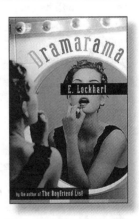

who has redefined herself as Sayde, is not so fortunate, squabbling with roommates and directors alike and learning that she is not as talented as she had thought she was. It's hard for her not to be jealous of Demi, and their friendship will be put to the test when the two are caught drinking on campus. Lockhart has done a beautiful job of capturing the vivid, larger-than-life personalities and inherent drama of, well, a *drama* camp. There is a great deal of information about the theater in the fast-paced story that lends it a nice air of verisimilitude, which will prove irresistible to teen theater buffs. **GA**

London, Alex

Proxy

Philomel, 2013. 384 p. ISBN: 9780399257766

THE SETTING IS A POSTAPOCALYPTIC dystopia where rigid class lines separate the ruling one percent from the rest of society, the underclass. Knox, sixteen, was born into the elite class. As such, he can have whatever he wants: the latest tech-

nology, the coolest cars, the trendiest clothing. Knox can also do whatever he wants, and if that gets him in trouble, he has a proxy—a member of the underclass—as a whipping boy to take his punishments. As a proxy for bad boy Knox, Syd has paid for Knox's misdeeds in physical punishment and forced labor, but as a foundling, he has no family to shoulder the cost of raising him to adulthood, so the debt he owes his for-profit orphan home has been piling up with every meal he's eaten and every article of clothing he's outgrown. His decision to sign a proxy contract reflects his eagerness to pay off that debt; in two years Knox will turn eighteen and Syd's servitude will be over. But then Knox's reckless driving results in the death of his passenger, and Syd is suddenly looking at a ten-year prison sentence. Instead, he breaks his proxy contract and takes off. Syd is a gay action hero whose sexuality is only one facet of his character and whose story suddenly becomes a gripping dystopian mystery thriller. **GA**

Lurie, April
The Less-Dead
Delacorte Press, 2010. 229 p. ISBN: 9780385736756

SOMEONE IS KILLING HOMELESS GAY teens in Austin, Texas. Clues suggest a religious connection. Might the murderer be someone from Noah's church? This is one question that Noah's father, famous radio personality the Bible Answer Guy, can't answer. When Will, a gay teen who Noah has befriended, is murdered, Noah (who is straight) decides to find the truth for himself. And, yes, it's a foolhardy idea, but it does keep the pages

turning. In *The Less-Dead* Lurie has written a combination mystery and cautionary tale about the uneasy relationship between homosexuality and religion. To her credit she is fair to both sides of this sensitive equation while acknowledging there are many religions that do regard homosexuality as sinful. Indeed, in an appendix she discusses the various Bible passages that are often cited by those who regard it as such. Clearly, she does not. Those who want to read other novels about this subject should see Alex Sanchez's *The God Box*, Mark Hardy's *Nothing Pink*, and Michael Cart's *My Father's Scar*. **GA**

Mac, Carrie

Crush

Orca, 2006. 106 p. ISBN: 9781551435268

WHEN HER PARENTS, LONGTIME HIPPIES and organic farmers, decide to celebrate their thirtieth anniversary by traveling to Thailand to help build a school, seventeen-year-old Hope arrives in New York to spend the summer with her older sister, Joy, a self-absorbed underwear model with an unpleasant disposition, a modest coke habit, and—in Hope—an unwelcome younger sister crashing in her living room. In short order Hope fortuitously lands a job as a live-in nanny for a lesbian couple with twins. And then she meets nineteen-year-old Nat, a "blond-dreadlocked skater girl" lesbian who works at a nearby bike shop. She has long legs and a terrific smile, and Hope finds her attractive—no, more than attractive, *way* more. "Ok, so I obviously have a crush on Nat. I might be new to the whole girl thing, but I'm not new to how being crushed out feels. This is a crush of the highest order." So does Nat feel the same way about Hope? Well, what do *you* think? A novel in the Orca Soundings series, this is a fast-paced coming-of-age story told in Hope's fresh and quirky voice that will have wide appeal to reluctant teen readers. **GA, QC**

Magoon, Kekla

37 Things I Love
(in No Particular Order)

Henry Holt, 2012. 218 p. ISBN: 9780805094657

WHEN ELLIS WAS THIRTEEN, HER father suffered severe head injuries in a workplace accident and slipped into a coma. He's been on life support ever since. Ellis is now fifteen and her father is still comatose, but she continues to make daily visits to his bedside where she talks to him about her daily life, from ordinary events to the thoughts she shares with no one else. Certainly not her mother, who is struggling with single parenthood, and certainly not her self-absorbed best friend, Abby. There was a time when Ellis had two close friends, Abby and Cara. But at some point, Abby began to exclude Cara and insisted that Ellis follow suit. Ellis has never known why this happened, but Abby has continued to call the shots, and Ellis has never questioned Abby's judgment. One evening all three end up at the same party, and while the feckless Abby gets drunk, Ellis and Cara begin to talk. Their former intimacy returns as Ellis learns that Abby's determination to end their friendship with Cara was in fact her homophobic response to Cara's coming out process, of which Ellis knew nothing. The new trust between Cara and Ellis enables each to see the kindred spirit in the other. This is a fine exploration of friendship that is restored via honesty. **HV**

Malloy, Brian
Twelve Long Months
Scholastic, 2008. 320 p. ISBN: 9780439877619

MALLOY, AUTHOR OF THE ALEX Award–winning adult novel *Year of Ice*, writes in the LGBT tradition of the straight girl falling madly in love with a swoon-worthy boy only to discover that the object of her affection is gay. In this case the girl is brainy Molly who is headed for Columbia University on a scholarship. She is elated to learn that her lab partner, the dreamy but enigmatic Mark, is also moving to New York—well, to New Jersey but close enough for regular visits. It is when he asks if he can crash at her dorm room one evening that she learns, to her sorrow, that he is gay. Happily the two become friends and, though that friendship will be tested, it survives to good effect. Though, at 320 pages, the novel is longer than it needs to be, it is well written, the characters are appealing, and the ending, satisfying. **HV**

Mazer, Norma Fox
The Missing Girl
HarperTeen, 2008. 284 p. ISBN: 9780066237770

MAZER'S EXCELLENT PSYCHOLOGICAL THRILLER tells the story of the abduction of eleven-year-old Autumn Herbert by an unnamed man who keeps her prisoner in his house. How can she escape? Will she escape? The answers will be forthcoming in time, but until then readers are left in white-knuckled suspense. The gay content in the book is definitely secondary. Mim, one of Autumn's older sisters, is a lesbian who quietly comes out to Beauty, the oldest of the five Herbert sisters. That nothing more is made of Mim's sexual identity might disqualify this title from our bibliography except that more and more books with LGBTQ content feature secondary characters, like Mim, who just happen to be gay and whose sexuality is treated casually. This gay visibility trope reflects the gradual but continuing acceptance of homosexuality in contemporary US society. Art, it seems, *can* imitate life to good ends. **GA**

McMahon, Jennifer
My Tiki Girl
Dutton, 2008. 246 p. ISBN: 9780525479437

FIFTEEN-YEAR-OLD MAGGIE KELLER thinks of herself as a "Frankenstein girl" because the bones in her right leg are held together with screws and a metal rod, leaving her with a stiff-legged limp. The injury is the result of an automobile accident that killed her mother, an accident that Maggie blames on herself. Maggie is largely friendless—her old friends having abandoned her as "a downer"—but then she meets the new girl in class, "dark, intense, freaky outcast poet girl Dahlia." The two girls soon fall in love and begin a clandestine relationship, clandestine, that is, until Maggie's former best friend observes the girls in what she sees as a kiss and outs them at school. In the meantime Dahlia's schizophrenic mother discovers the girls in a genuinely compromising situation, orders Maggie out of the house and then contacts Maggie's father, who forbids his daughter to see Dahlia again. Is this the end of their relationship? McMahon's first novel for young adults (she's an established adult author) breaks no new ground and is a tad melodramatic (in addition to Dahlia's mother's mental illness, one of the girls' friends lives in a cave to avoid his drunken, battering father) but is, nevertheless, heartfelt and the girls' relationship is sensitively and sympathetically handled. **HV**

Moore, Perry
Hero
Hyperion, 2007. 432 p. ISBN: 9781423101963

MOORE, PRODUCER OF THE NARNIA films, has written a novel that echoes classic superhero comics. Thom Creed, a teenage basketball star, has several secrets: one is that he has a superpower (the capacity to heal) and another, he's gay. His secretiveness is due to his father, a discredited former superhero named Major Might who now hates the ilk and is a homophobe to boot. Thom's life gets complicated when he is made a probationary member of the League, an X-Men-like organization, and is assigned duty with other novice heroes. Pretty soon the young crusaders find themselves tasked with saving the world, while Thom has an equally daunting personal task: he is committed to coming out but cannot predict what this will mean to his relationships with both his father and the League. Though the story has flaws—it is somewhat derivative and predictable—*Hero* is nevertheless significant as the first and only non-graphic novel to feature a teenage gay superhero. **HV, GA**

Moskowitz, Hannah

Gone, Gone, Gone

Simon Pulse, 2012. 272 p. ISBN: 9781442407534

ANOTHER INTENSE READING EXPERIENCE from Moskowitz, *Gone, Gone, Gone* is the story of two boys who are living in Washington, DC, during the 2002 beltway sniper attacks and struggling with their budding relationship. Craig is hurting from his breakup with his ex boyfriend Cody and deals with the pain by obsessively rescuing and sheltering a host of stray animals (four dogs, five cats, one bird, three rabbits, and a guinea pig!). Lio—the new kid in town, who sports a head of multicolored hair—mourns his twin brother's death from cancer while he himself is a cancer survivor. He is dealing with his loss and his feelings for Craig in therapy. When Craig wakes up one morning to discover his animals are gone, he turns to Lio for help in recovering them. The story is told, in alternating chapters, from each boy's perspective as they discuss and debate the emotional fallout from national tragedies and their growing romantic attachment. A quiet but intense love story that invites discussion and debate. **GA**

Moskowitz, Hannah

Marco Impossible

Roaring Brook Press, 2013. 249 p. ISBN: 9781596437210

STEPHEN AND MARCO HAVE REACHED the end of eighth grade and a parting of the ways as they head off to different high schools. Though best friends, the two have many points of difference: Marco is an only child, gay, and short; Stephen is one of six siblings, straight, and is not exactly tall, but getting there. However, their friendship has been forged in steel by their longtime and mostly successful partnership as amateur detectives. ("We've apprehended more cellphone thieves and

returned more lost puppies . . . than most thirteen-year-olds could ever dream of.") Now two new mysteries have come to their attention: First, does Marco's longtime crush, Benji, return his feelings? Second, who is responsible for the escalating homophobic attacks on Marco (anonymous notes, vandalized locker, what next?)? Stephen is narrator and faithful sidekick to the irrepressible Marco. As Stephen says, "nothing is straightforward when Marco's involved . . . and when you have a best friend like Marco, he is always, always involved." The rapidly moving story covers two days of high-speed anxiety as they skirt the law, flout authority, and flee from and then capture bullies. Can a short novel vividly evoke both pain and hilarity? Exasperation and admiration? Aggravation and delight? This one can. **GA**

Moskowitz, Hannah
Teeth
Simon Pulse, 2013. 246 p. ISBN: 9781442465329

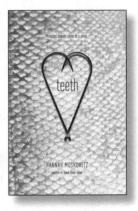

TEENAGE RUDY'S YOUNGER BROTHER HAS cystic fibrosis, and his parents have moved the family to a remote island, home to fish that have magical healing powers. At first a lonely Rudy believes he is the only teenager on the island. But then he meets his lovely neighbor Diana and the two begin an affectionate relationship. However, it is her older brother, a half-boy, half-fish who calls himself Teeth, with whom Rudy forms an intense emotional relationship. The central problem here is a painful one: Teeth lives in the sea and believes that his mission is protecting the magical fish whom he regards as his siblings. Accordingly he cuts the fishermen's nets and they, in retribution, manage to regularly catch and beat him. Rudy tries to save him but soon realizes that if Teeth is successful, the source of fish will dry up and his brother may die. How can he manage to save both Teeth and his brother? Moskowitz's novel of magical realism is compelling but often hard to read because of its intense feeling of foreboding; the reader imagines that terrible things will happen to Teeth, a supposition that is painful but not necessarily true. The relationship between the two boys is somewhat ambiguous, but most readers will believe that the two are in love with each other and that one or both of them is gay. Once read, this unusual novel is hard to forget. **GA**

Mowry, Jess
Babylon Boyz
Simon & Schuster, 1997. 192 p. ISBN: 9780689825927

THE BABYLON BOYZ ARE WYATT, Dante, and Pook, three African American inner-city teens in Oakland, longtime friends who come upon an abandoned suit-case full of cocaine. On the one hand, the suitcase represents life-threatening danger at the hands of the dealers desperate to retrieve it. On the other hand, the contents of the suitcase could pay for Dante's much-needed surgery to fix his bad heart, the result of his pre-natal exposure to crack cocaine. This is urban fiction at its grittiest, a tangled and suspenseful tale of young teens who suddenly find themselves in life-threatening trouble with few resources but their street smarts and mutual loyalty that is unsentimentally solid. All three are vividly realized char-acters. Pook is particularly memorable as a gay teen whose struggle is not with his sexual identity but with finding the resources to help him realize his dream of becoming a medical doctor. This is still one of the few YA novels with LGBTQ con-tent featuring gay African Americans. **GA**

Murdock, Catherine Gilbert
Dairy Queen
Houghton Mifflin, 2006. 274 p. ISBN: 9780618863358

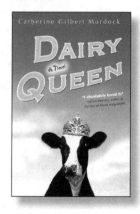

DJ IS A WORKER AND it's a good thing too, for—since her father hurt his hip—she's had to do virtually all the work on the family farm. To help out, a family friend and coach of DJ's school's football archrival sends his quarterback, Brian, to work on the farm. Antagonists at first, the two teens gradually become friends. When that friendship appears to be turning into something more, DJ's best friend, Amber, becomes jealous and finally admits that she is in love with DJ. In the meantime DJ has become Brian's trainer, but when she decides to go out for football herself (she makes the team!), Brian feels betrayed and there is a dramatic encounter on the football field. The gay content is fairly minor—DJ and Amber have a temporary falling out in the wake of Amber's confession—but well and sensitively handled. The larger ques-tion, in the context of the novel, is whether DJ and Brian will be able to put aside their feelings of betrayal and reconcile. Readers of this excellent novel will be cheering for them. **HV**

Murdock, Catherine Gilbert
The Off Season
Houghton Mifflin, 2007. 288 p. ISBN: 9780547349411

THE SEQUEL to Dairy Queen. **GA**

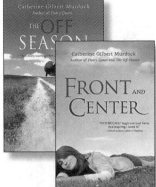

Murdock, Catherine Gilbert
Front and Center
Houghton Mifflin, 2009. 276 p. ISBN: 9780618959822

VOLUME 3 in the Dairy Queen trilogy. **GA**

Myracle, Lauren
Kissing Kate
Dutton, 2003. 176 p. ISBN: 9780525469179

KATE AND LISSA HAVE BEEN close friends since they were twelve. Now sixteen, Lissa tells the story of their friendship, so suddenly disrupted by one surprising event. Actually, Lissa's never really understood why the she and Kate became friends in the first place. They hadn't known each other until middle school. But then after school one day they just started talking. Lissa remembers asking Kate why. Kate's response, "'You were different from what I expected. . . . In a good way, Lissa. You know that.' But I didn't," Lissa thinks, "not anymore. Not since two weeks ago when Kate leaned in to kiss me and like an idiot I kissed her back. All I knew now was that nothing lasted forever and that being 'different' felt the same as being alone." Lissa wants to talk about "it," but Kate clearly wants to forget their kiss ever happened. Yes, Lissa has a job, a life, and friends of her own, but as the weeks drag on, she keeps coming back to that kiss. Not to the kiss itself, exactly, but to the distance that Kate has put between them since then. Will that kiss mean something about either or both of their future lives? **HV**

Myracle, Lauren
Shine
Abrams Amulet, 2011. 357 p. ISBN: 9780810984172

MYRACLE'S HARD-HITTING NOVEL opens with a newspaper account of a horrific incident in tiny Black Creek, North Carolina: Patrick Truman, a local teen, is found

tied to the gasoline pump at the convenience store where he works. Barely alive, the boy is badly beaten and unconscious with the gasoline nozzle protruding from his mouth and the words "Suck on this faggot" scrawled in blood across his chest. Yes, Patrick is openly gay but widely accepted locally, so who could have perpetrated such a vile hate crime? Cat, a former friend of Patrick determines to find out. The story then becomes a compelling, character-driven mystery. Patrick lies unconscious in an area hospital, but his silent presence is everywhere in the story. While examining one specific incident, Myracle's compelling novel has universal application to hate crimes everywhere and the irrational impulses that drive their perpetrators. Although the ending smacks of wish fulfillment, *Shine* remains a significant contribution to readers' understanding of the unthinkable. **GA**

Ness, Patrick

More Than This

Candlewick Press, 2013. 480 p. ISBN: 9780763662585

THE STORY BEGINS WITH THE death by drowning of sixteen-year-old Seth, who then wakes up—nearly naked and swathed in bandages—lying in front of the English home where he spent his childhood before his family moved to the United States. The house and the entire neighborhood are eerily empty and seem to have been deserted for quite some time. In fact, as Seth explores, he discovers he is apparently the only person left alive in whatever world he is in. Is this the future? Is it hell? He doesn't know. But then he encounters two other young people who appear providentially just in time to save him from a mysterious, dark figure they call "The Driver." As the three attempt to make sense of their lives, readers learn about Seth's previous life, including his love relationship with his best friend, Gudmund, through his dreams. There is a great deal of page-turning action in this suspenseful novel, but for some readers the most fascinating part will be the brain-teasing intimations of a multiverse that it invokes. Another winner from the acclaimed author of A *Monster Calls* and The Chaos Walking trilogy. **GA**

Papademetriou, Lisa and Chris Tebbetts

M or F?

Razorbill, 2005. 296 p. ISBN: 9781595140340

SO WHO'S TYPING IN THE chat room, an M or an F? Well, it's complicated. See, Frannie has a crush on this cute guy named Jeff but she's too shy and nervous to talk to him, so her gay BFF, Marcus, suggests she chat with him online. Sounds like a good idea, but Frannie thinks she's a lousy writer, so Marcus steps in to help her. And soon he's writing, a la Cyrano de Bergerac, all her chat messages for her. Then he realizes he's starting to fall for Jeff himself and, without Frannie's knowing it, starts sending messages to Jeff as her. This is the beginning of a very tangled web, indeed, as misunderstandings and mistaken identities abound in this lighthearted romance that saves its biggest surprises for its (happy) ending. The happiest part of the novel, though, is its depiction of Marcus as an out gay teen whose sexual identity is accepted and whose life is mercifully missing the Sturm und Drang that historically visited the lives of gay teens. Now *that's* a happy ending! **GA**

Peck, Dale

Sprout

Bloomsbury, 2009. 277 p. ISBN: 9781599901602

WHY IS SIXTEEN-YEAR-OLD DANIEL BRADFORD'S nickname "Sprout"? Hint: he dyes his hair green. Clearly a nonconformist in his tiny Kansas town, the boy is a gifted writer, and his English-teacher mentor is determined to enter him in the statewide essay contest, which he just might win—if only he doesn't write about his being gay. Speaking of which, Sprout is having a purely physical relationship with former bully Ian until an appealing new boy, Ty, arrives in town and suddenly a more satisfying relationship appears within reach. If only, that is, Sprout's high-powered friend Ruthie will stop insisting the two come out with their relationship. An established adult author and literary critic, Peck brings a keen wit and intelligence to his first YA novel, a satisfyingly character-driven work of literary fiction. **HV**

Peters, Julie Anne

Between Mom and Jo

Little, Brown, 2006. 232 p. ISBN: 9780316067102

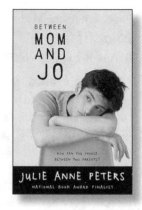

NICK HAS TWO MOMS—HIS BIRTH mother and her partner, Jo. He loves them both with all his heart, but growing up with lesbian parents has not been easy as he's been subjected to teasing and verbal abuse from other students and even from one of his teachers. If this were all the book is about, it would be a fairly predictable read. But Peters has more in mind. The story comes alive when Nick's two moms' relationship ends bitterly and the fourteen-year-old is caught between the two women. He longs to live with Jo, but as a lesbian she has never been able to formally adopt him, so his birth mother has full custody. Things go from bad to worse when his mom starts a new relationship and refuses to let him see Jo or even talk with her on the phone. How can such a situation possibly be resolved? Peters manages this beautifully in what may be her best book to date, certainly one of her most heartfelt. High marks to her for plausibility too. Every aspect of her plot rings true, and, as a character, Nick is definitely a keeper. **GA**

Peters, Julie Anne

grl2grl

Little, Brown, 2007. 160 p. ISBN: 9780316013437

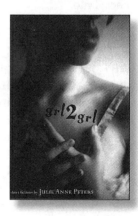

PETERS'S COLLECTION OF TEN SHORT stories focuses on young women dealing with their sexual or gender identity and the attendant challenges and problems that confront them. One girl, who describes herself as a "stone cold butch" is being sexually abused by her father; another girl, more innocuously, has a crush on a teacher; another, a male-to-female transgender character, is assaulted and still another agonizes over attending a gay-straight alliance meeting. The stories—all told in the first person—cover a broad spectrum of emotional and social issues but all have in common their integrity and authenticity. This excellent collection by a leading voice in LGBTQ literature is one of the few LGBT short story collections (see also Ellen Wittlinger's *What's in a Name* and Marion Dane Bauer's *Am I Blue?*). **HA, GA, QC**

Peters, Julie Anne

It's Our Prom (So Deal with It)

Little, Brown, 2012. 352 p. ISBN: 9780316131582

WHEN AZURE COMPLAINS THAT HER school's freaks, geeks, and other assorted outsiders are neither welcome at the senior prom nor interested in attending even if they were, she finds herself pressed into serving on the event's planning committee and is determined to fashion an alternative experience. Also on the committee are her BFFs, Luke and Radhika. Complicating matters is the fact that Azure is a lesbian, Luke is bisexual, and both are smitten with Radhika, who is straight. In the meantime Luke is serving as author, producer, director, and star of an autobiographical play about his coming-out experience. Many complications ensue, most comic, a few more serious. More lighthearted than many of her other novels, *It's Our Prom* finds Peters in a sunny humor while still addressing issues such as bisexuality, coming out, and the agonies and ecstasies of romantic love. Though hardly great literature, the result lives up to its good intentions and gives readers a realistic look at contemporary LGBTQ life. **GA, QC**

Peters, Julie Anne

Keeping You a Secret

Little, Brown, 2003. 252 p. ISBN: 9780316009850

HOLLAND JAEGER IS HAVING A success-filled senior year and it's barely even started: she's student council president and a member of the swim team, she has a good-looking boyfriend, and she appears to be living out her mother's dreams for her future. But her life is turned upside down when she meets Cece, a new student who saunters into school wearing a T-shirt emblazoned with "IMRU?" and a rainbow triangle. Holland is impressed by Cece's boldness but even more by her own immediate attraction to Cece—and the attraction is definitely mutual. "The electricity between us was palpable. Visible, almost. And dangerous. . . . She hadn't touched me, but God, I wanted her to." At first, they keep their romance a secret to avoid the kind of social rejection that drove Cece to switch schools, but as their clandestine romance becomes more intense, Holland's friends and family—and, oh yes, her boyfriend—grow increasingly suspicious of the time the girls spend together. And when Holland finally decides to tell the truth and come out to her parents, her mother responds by giving her daughter two minutes to vacate the premises. This compelling survival story is Peters's first novel. **HV, QC**

Peters, Julie Anne

Luna

Little, Brown, 2004. 248 p. ISBN: 9780316011273

LUNA IS A GIRL WHO can only be seen by moonlight. During the day she is Liam, a teenage boy who is secretly male-to-female transgender. Regan, his younger sister and only confidant, tells his story. "It must be horrible to be in the wrong body, to have this dual identity. Why couldn't people just be accepted for who they were?" Depressed and nearly suicidal from living a lie, Liam decides it's time to begin his transition, it's time for Luna to emerge into the daylight—with Regan's help, willing or not. "It's always about my brother," she thinks, overwhelmed by his expectations. "My brother was a black hole in my universe. He was sucking the life right out of me." Nevertheless she continues to help him . . . until he can help himself to become his real self, to find a place where Luna can be accepted for who she is. Short-listed for the National Book Award, *Luna*, though sometimes painful to read, is the first young adult novel to feature a transgender character and, thus, to give a face to one of the last invisible minorities in the genre. **HV**

Peters, Julie Anne

Pretend You Love Me

Little, Brown, 2011. 304 p. ISBN: 9780316127417
(original title: **Far from Xanadu.***) Little, Brown,*
2005. 282 p. ISBN: 9780316159715

THE PROLIFIC PETERS FOCUSES ON gender and sexual ambiguity in this novel about Mike, the first-person protagonist whom readers will initially presume is a boy. But not so. Despite the fact that Mike (born Mary Elizabeth) pumps iron and plays softball, she is very much a girl. She's also an out lesbian, though not as assertively out as her male best friend, Jamie. When bad girl Xanadu moves to their small Kansas town, Mike falls head over heels in love with her—even though

Xanadu is straight. The girl, who has been sent to live with relatives after being busted for dealing drugs, gives mixed messages to keep Mike holding on. In the meantime Mike must deal with a clutch of real-life problems. Her father has killed himself, her morbidly obese mother has lapsed into silence, and her apparently no-good brother has run the family plumbing business into the ground. Will Mike decide to take over the business or accept a softball scholarship to college? Peters does a nice job with her theme and an even better one with her unusual setting, a small town that accepts the two gay teens. "I never, for one day, felt judged or excluded or persecuted in Coalton," Mike thinks. Add to this the (for LGBTQ literature) unusual theme of gay-straight attraction, and you have another winner from Peters. **GA**

Peters, Julie Anne

She Loves You, She Loves You Not . . .

Little, Brown, 2011. 278 p. ISBN: 9780316078757

WHEN SEVENTEEN-YEAR-OLD ALYSSA'S homophobic father discovers she's a lesbian, he disowns her and sends her from Virginia to Colorado to live with her (straight) mother whom she scarcely knows. Alyssa finds it difficult to forgive her mother, Carley, for having abandoned her when she was an infant, but the two manage an uneasy relationship, which is not helped by the fact that Carley is an exotic dancer. Everyone in their small town knows Carley and automatically calls Alyssa "Carley's girl," making it difficult for her to be her own person. In the meantime she meets and falls in love with Finn, a girl who is an independent spirit and a rolling stone. Will the two manage to form a lasting relationship? And will Alyssa ever be able to effect a rapprochement with her unforgiving father? Peters has written anther fine novel with fully developed characters and a strong theme of independence that never gets in the way of a compelling and satisfying story. **HV**

Pierce, Tamora

The Will of the Empress

Scholastic, 2005. 550 p. ISBN: 9780545074551

THE FOUR YOUNG MAGES AND foster siblings whom readers met in Pierce's *The Circle of Magic* and The Circle Opens series return. Now sixteen and newly reunited after solo journeys, Daja, Tris, Briar, and Sandry must decide if they will close each other off from their telepathic connection. "As adults we keep our minds and our secrets hidden, and our wounds. It's safer." Sandry then discovers that the lands she holds for her relative the Empress Berenene of Namorn will be confiscated if she doesn't return home. Her three siblings duly accompany her to Namorn, where all find themselves virtual prisoners thanks to the will of the empress who refuses to let them—and Sandry's inheritance—go. The empress even attempts to force several arranged marriages on Sandry. In the meantime Daja discovers she is a "woman who loves women" and begins an affair with the empress's ward-

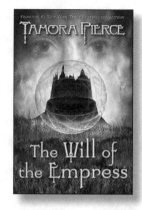

robe mistress. What will happen to the lovers, and will the four mages manage to escape? What do you think? Pierce brings a feminist sensibility to her epic tale of adventure, journeys, and court life that resonates with contemporary real life. Though this novel can stand alone, it is perhaps best understood in the context of the mages' earlier adventures. **HV**

Ripslinger, Jon

How I Fell in Love and Learned to Shoot Free Throws

Roaring Brook, 2003. 170 p. ISBN: 9780761318927

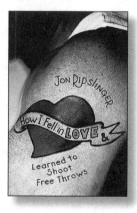

THE TIME IS NOW; the place is Iowa, a state with a long and storied history of girls' high school basketball. There's boys' basketball too, of course, but the girls' teams receive equal if not more attention from the media. Danny Henderson is devoted to Big River High School basketball, but his lack of free throw skill cost his team an otherwise close game and he doesn't want it to happen again. Angel McPherson (aka "Stone Angel") is the star of the school girls' basketball team—heck, she's probably the best women's basketball player in the state. And her free throws are just about perfect. Off the court she keeps to herself, but Danny has had a crush on her since she moved to Big River six months ago, and he really, really wants to improve his game. He gathers his nerve and asks her to help him. As it happens, she is looking for some pointers on rebounding, and the two decide to meet, but Danny's nerves get the better of him and he accidentally steps on and breaks her foot. Sheesh! Rumor has it that Angel's gay, and certainly she avoids all Danny's questions about her off-court life, but it's clear she likes kissing him. Both Danny and Angel are well-drawn and engaging characters, and their attraction has its moments, both painful and amusing. Readers will be rooting for both of them. **HV**

Rud, Jeff
Crossover
Orca, 2008. 170 p. ISBN: 9781551439815

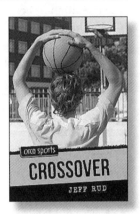

HOMOPHOBIA IS THE THEME OF this fast-paced sports story. When starting varsity basketball player Kyle Evans is cast as The Artful Dodger in his high school's production of the musical *Oliver*, his bullying teammate Ben Stillman sneers, "I thought you were supposed to be a basketball player, not one of the funny boys of the drama department." Kyle shakes off the insult, but his childhood friend and star of the show, Lukas, is routinely taunted and bullied for being gay, despite the fact that Lukas himself is not sure if he is gay or straight. Nevertheless, his locker is vandalized and, even worse, the sets for the show are trashed. Will the perpetrators be caught? Will Kyle be able to balance the demands of both basketball and drama? Though he sometimes paints with a very broad brush, author Rud has written an emotionally engaging story of teenagers confronting and overcoming stereotypes and homophobia. **HV**

Ruditis, Paul
Drama! Entrances and Exits
Simon Pulse, 2008. 242 p. ISBN: 9781416959069

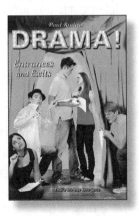

YES, THERE'S PLENTY OF DRAMA in *Drama!* The story is told by drama student Bryan Stark, who is elated when he is chosen to direct his friend Hope's play in Orion Academy's Fall One-Act Festival. But complications soon ensue. Playwright Hope is livid when her evil stepsister Belinda is chosen for a major role in the play and even more livid (livider?) when her other evil stepsister Alexis is selected to do the cast's hair. What next? Well, Bryan's former best friend, Drew, is still hardly speaking to him since Bryan was outed. What's up with that? And leading actress Sam's boyfriend, Eric, is unhappy at the chemistry between Sam and her leading man, Jason. And this is only the start. It turns out that Bryan's associate stage manager is also gay and seems to have eyes for him. Or maybe he's just trying to make Drew jealous. This drama aside, what about the real drama, the play? Will Bryan turn out to be a good director despite his problems with his cast and crew? Is all this drama over nothing . . . or something? Kids who like drama—both on and offstage—will enjoy this lighthearted romp, which handles its gay content with warmth and some welcome humor. This is the fourth and final volume in Ruditis's Drama series, which also includes *The Four Dorothys* (2007), *Everyone's a Critic* (2007), and *Show, Don't Tell* (2008). **GA**

Ryan, Patrick
Gemini Bites
Scholastic, 2011. 240 p. ISBN: 9780545221283

RYAN (*IN MIKE WE TRUST*), one of the more promising new voices in LGBTQ literature, tells the offbeat story of fraternal twin teens Kyle and Judy. The two have a less than loving relationship. Kyle calls Judy "The Monster," and she reciprocates by calling him "the boy who loves penises" (yes, he's gay). However, they have one thing in common: horror at the prospect of Garrett, a boy from their school, coming to live for a month with their family. Affecting a Goth persona (black clothes and eyeliner on one eye), Garrett steadfastly claims to be a vampire. Whether he is or not, the twins—as they get to know him—start to find him intriguing and then increasingly attractive. Does he feel the same about them? Much cheerier than it sounds, the novel offers an engaging look at contemporary gay teen life, while candidly acknowledging that teens are sexual beings. **GA**

Ryan, P. E.
In Mike We Trust
HarperTeen, 2009. 321 p. ISBN: 9780060858131

AS A 5'2" FIFTEEN-YEAR-OLD, Garth is understandably tired of being a growth-spurt late bloomer, and he's *really* tired of living a lie. When he tells his mother he's gay, she insists he keep it a secret because she doesn't want him to get hurt. Because of his father's relatively recent death, Garth is loath to make his mother's life more worrisome, but things are getting complicated.

Uncle Mike, his father's long-estranged identical twin brother, unexpectedly arrives and moves in. Then Garth falls for Adam, who is openly gay but appears to have a credibility problem in other areas of his life. Garth's lies get increasingly tangled when Mike involves him in some iffy fund-raising activities that he must keep secret from his mother. On the plus side, Mike has intuited Garth's sexuality and takes him to a gay bookstore so he can read about the lives of gay men. Ryan has created several memorable characters here, and the plot rings true in a "well, if something like that *did* happen, it would probably happen like that" way. Mike is a surprisingly likeable flimflam man, and Garth's developing relationship with Adam is emotionally engaging. **HV**

Ryan, P. E.

Saints of Augustine

HarperTempest, 2007. 320 p. ISBN: 9780061975394

SAM AND CHARLIE, BOTH SEVENTEEN, are ex best friends. Between them they have a plateful of problems the reader discovers in chapters that alternate between the two. Charlie's mother, for example, has died, and he and his father cope by self-medicating, the father with alcohol and Charlie with pot. Sam has also lost a parent, his father, who has moved out to live with a male "roommate." Sam, who is attracted to a boy named Justin, is increasingly concerned he might be gay like his father, a concern exacerbated by the fact that his mother's new boyfriend is blatantly homophobic. While Sam is attempting to deal with these problems, Charlie's life is falling apart: his girlfriend dumps him because of his drug habit, which has put him dangerously in debt to his violence-disposed dealer. Things come to a head the night the drug dealer trashes Charlie's car while Sam's mother inadvertently witnesses her son's first gay kiss. Both Sam and Charlie are in desperate need of a friend. Can the two reconcile and restore their friendship? Ryan's first novel for young adults is a character-driven work of fiction that expertly captures both teenage angst and the possibilities of emotional recovery. **HV**

Ryan, Sara

Empress of the World

Viking, 2001. 213 p. ISBN: 9780142500590

FIFTEEN-YEAR-OLD NIC (SHORT FOR NICOLA) is spending eight weeks living on a college campus as a student at the Siegel Institute Summer Program for Gifted

Youth. There she plans to immerse herself in the study of archeology, a longtime interest that might point her toward a future career. Her peers are an interestingly quirky lot, and she quickly settles in with a small group of sharp-witted nonconformists, one of whom is Battle, a fierce and beautiful honey-haired Southerner, for whom Nic feels an immediate attraction. The feeling is, happily, mutual, and despite the fact that this feeling is new to both of them, their closeness increases with a refreshing lack of Sturm und Drang from their friends or each other. The summer is a heady mix of independence and intellectual challenge, as Nic and her friends find kindred spirits and get a glimpse of some future possibilities their lives may hold for them. This is one of the first YA titles to include bisexuality. **HV, GA**

Ryan, Tom
Way to Go
Orca, 2012. 214 p. ISBN: 9781459800779

"BY THE TIME I WAS SEVENTEEN," Danny says, "I had a lot of practice at keeping secrets." One of these is that he might be gay. He's deeply closeted but still worries if people in his small hometown are beginning to "say things" about him. The last thing on earth he wants to be is gay, he resolutely tells himself, but his body refuses to cooperate with his brain. Perhaps if he just finds the right girl? And then he meets Lisa, who looks like she might be. At first he thinks she's the one but decides that if, in fact, she doesn't turn him on, his only option would be to move away—far away. In the meantime, however, his mother gets him a job in a new restaurant and before you can say "sous chef," he's become one and—to his father's displeasure—is considering going to culinary school to become a chef! Canadian author Ryan does a good job of mixing Danny's discovery of his sexual identity with his discovery of an exciting career opportunity. In the end Danny has come out to two of his friends—though not to his family—and is preparing to apply for culinary school and a promising future. **HV**

Saenz, Benjamin Alire

Aristotle and Dante Discover the Secrets of the Universe

Simon & Schuster, 2012. 359 p. ISBN: 9781442408920

SET IN EL PASO, TEXAS, in the late 1980's, this Printz Honor and Pura Belpre Award-winning title charts a year-and-a-half in the lives of two fifteen-year-old Mexican-American boys, Ari and Dante, who are unlikely best friends. Unlikely because of their many differences: Ari is moody and introspective, closely guarding a family secret (his older brother is in prison); Dante, on the other hand, is openly gay, often ebullient, light to Ari's dark. Together the boys are like two halves making a whole. The two meet when Dante offers to teach Ari how to swim and quickly bond, though they come from very different class backgrounds. Each has a loving and supportive family who connect when Ari saves Dante's life but is seriously injured in the process. This, plus a year spent apart (Dante's father becomes a visiting professor at the University of Chicago) helps the boys to re-examine their relationship. What will this mean to their friendship? Might it become deeper and richer? Or might it end? The answers are realistic and satisfying. Told in Ari's first person voice, this psychologically acute story is a beautiful examination of adolescent friendship that will resonate with readers long after the final page. **HV, GA**

St. James, James

Freak Show

Dutton, 2007. 304 p. ISBN: 9781440651557

ST. JAMES, AUTHOR OF *DISCO BLOODBATH* and himself a longtime fixture on the gay disco scene, makes his debut in the world of YA literature to outrageously good effect. His protagonist, seventeen-year-old Billy Bloom, is a teenage drag queen whose life in Connecticut is quite fabulous, thank you very much. However, events conspire to send him to Florida to live with his conservative father and attend the equally conservative Dwight D. Eisenhower Academy. Horrors! But Billy, naïve, clueless, and undaunted shows up for his first day at the new school in full pirate regalia—but that has *nothing* on the swamp queen gown he will appear in later. Needless to say, his fellow students are at first nonplussed, then outraged, and finally, violent, and Billy winds up in the hospital. But payback time is coming, and he decides to run for prom queen. Along the way he finds a most unlikely protector and boyfriend (okay, it's the school's popular football hero). As a character, Billy is sui generis; there's no one else quite like him in the world of YA and his over-the-top adventures are at once hilarious and touching. Though not without its controversial elements, *Freak Show* is, in the final analysis, a fabulous charmer. **GA**

Salat, Cristina
Living in Secret
Bantam, 1993. 192 p. ISBN: 9780916020026

THE OPENING SENTENCE OF THIS middle-grade novel immediately grabs the reader: "In the middle of the night my mother comes to steal me away." When the parents of Amelia, the story's narrator and protagonist, divorce, her father demands sole custody of his five-year-old daughter, arguing that his former wife's "lesbian lifestyle" makes her an unfit parent. The family court judge agrees, and Amelia's time with her mother has been limited ever since. Amelia, now eleven, longs to live with her mother, Claire, and her mother's partner, Janie, so when her father restricts Amelia's time with her mother still further, Claire and Janie conclude that drastic action is needed, and the three make a clandestine escape to San Francisco to start new "living in secret" lives as family law fugitives. Claire, Janie, and Amelia become Kathy, Megan, and Julie Dreisden, a small and undocumented family facing financial and social hardships. Claire and Janie find low-wage jobs, and Amelia becomes a homeschooled twelve-year-old with a cover story (she's a low-achieving student preparing for middle school with a private tutor). Amelia is unhappily isolated from her peers, but when she makes a new friend the pleasure of companionship must be weighed against the potential harm that self-disclosure could bring to her family. Current-day lesbian mothers are less likely to face custody battles like Claire's, but the author effectively communicates the difficulties once common in the lives of LGBT parents and their children. A riveting read. **HV, QC**

Sanchez, Alex
Boyfriends with Girlfriends
Simon & Schuster, 2011. 224 p. ISBN: 9781416937739

INNOVATIVE LAMBDA AWARD-WINNING author Sanchez explores a seldom-covered topic in this intriguing novel: bisexuality. Sergio and Lance meet online and when they arrange their first date, Lance discovers that Sergio is bisexual. While definitely attracted, Lance is not sure he can handle Sergio's bisexuality or if he even believes bisexuality is a real condition of being. Meanwhile the boys' two best friends, Allie and Kimiko, who have come along on the first date for moral support, find themselves attracted to each other. This is not a problem for openly gay Kimiko, but Allie, who has always regarded herself as being straight, is not so sure. How the teens will handle their respective amatory situations is the stuff of another engaging novel from the talented Sanchez. Give him high marks for bringing some welcome and, for YA fiction, unusual insight into the often cloudy issue of bisexuality. **GA, QC**

Sanchez, Alex
Getting It
Simon & Schuster, 2006. 224 p. ISBN: 9781416908968

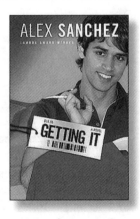

"FIFTEEN AND STILL A VIRGIN," Sanchez writes, "Carlos Amoroso wanted more than anything to get a girlfriend—and hopefully get laid." Not just any girlfriend, mind you, but Roxy Rodriguez, the popular and sexy cheerleader who doesn't even know he's alive. What to do? Carlos dithers, and then he has an aha moment and decides to get a makeover. In a nod to the TV series "Queer Eye for the Straight Guy," who better to do that than Sal, the gay guy at school? Sal reluctantly agrees but at a price: he wants Carlos to help him start a Gay-Straight Alliance at their school. Gulp. Will that mean everybody—especially his best friends—might conclude that Carlos is gay too? Lambda Award–winner Sanchez writes a lighthearted love story with a twist, in the process demystifying homosexuality for straight readers and, in Sal, creating a non-stereotypical—and even exemplary—role model. Though a touch didactic, the novel is a quick, engaging read. **GA**

Sanchez, Alex
The God Box
Simon & Schuster, 2007. 272 p. ISBN: 9781416909002

HIGH SCHOOL SENIOR PAUL and his friend Angie have been an item for years, but when Manuel, an openly gay boy, moves to Paul's small Texas town, Paul is dismayed by the attraction he feels, especially since his conservative church condemns homosexuality. But as it happens, Manuel is also religious and, in slightly didactic conversations, attempts to counter their church's teachings about homosexuality and gradually opens Paul up to new ways of thinking about religion . . . and himself. "I'm on that new path now," Paul reflects, "learning to love and accept myself as God created me." As a result, he also comes to embrace his Mexican-American identity and reclaims his birth name, Pablo, which he had changed to Paul to be "more American." Sanchez writes with candor, conviction, and compassion as he dramatizes the plight of teens who struggle to manage their homosexuality and their deeply felt religious beliefs. Readers who enjoy this will also want to read *Nothing Pink* by Mark Hardy. **GA, HV**

Sanchez, Alex
Rainbow Boys
Simon & Schuster, 2001. 256 p. ISBN: 9780689857706

JASON, KYLE, AND NELSON ARE three gay high school students whose lives include Rainbow Youth meetings at a community center and a campaign for a Gay-Straight Alliance in their high school. The story is told from the alternating perspectives of the three classmates, each of whom is wrestling with issues of sexual orientation and personal survival. Jason, a high school jock with a longtime girlfriend, is struggling to come out to himself. Kyle, a shy and intelligent ugly duckling, accepts his own gay identity, but what to do about his seemingly hopeless crush on Jason? And finally, there is Nelson, Kyle's flamboyant best friend whose multicolored hair, multi-pierced ears, and camp sensibility reflect his in-your-face identity as "queer and proud." These are the rainbow boys, all heroes of their own lives, and this collective narrative of three gay teen protagonists who are friends is downright revolutionary. Readers see the world from the boys' perspectives as they move in and out of a queer community via Rainbow Youth meetings and as they hang out after school, eating brownies, doing math homework, and looking forward to the large and interesting world that awaits them after high school. **HV, GA, QC**

Sanchez, Alex
Rainbow High
Simon & Schuster, 2003. 247 p. ISBN: 9780689854774

JASON, KYLE, AND NELSON ARE midway through their senior year and the Gay-Straight Alliance they had campaigned for is now a reality. This is the second in the three-book Rainbow Boys series, and as before, the story is told from the alternating perspectives of the three classmates, each of whom is wrestling with issues of sexual orientation and personal survival. Kyle's current life, for example, is somewhat rough, as he comes out to his swim coach and team and has to deal with both the coach's intense discomfort and the homophobia of some of his teammates. His future, however, is bright: he's been accepted to Princeton. But boyfriend Jason will be staying put at the local college: what will the separation mean for their relationship? In the meantime Jason's own decision to come out to his basketball team goes surprisingly smoothly, due in large part to the model his coach provides; nevertheless, the media attention Jason receives puts his basketball scholarship in jeopardy. And Nelson? Well, Nelson is dating Jeremy, a college student who is good-looking, intelligent, and HIV positive. So Nelson and his mother are having a series of dramatic arguments about the health risk of getting involved with Jeremy. Each of the three teens' lives is a work in progress, with the accompanying excitement and anxiety that comes with change. ("Every day I ask myself, What's going to happen next? And I just hope I don't screw it all up.") If they haven't already, readers will want to read the other two books in this well-received series. An appendix with information about eight LGBTQ organizations and youth advocates is included. **HV, QC**

Sanchez, Alex
Rainbow Road
Simon & Schuster, 2005. 242 p. ISBN: 9780689865657

THE THIRD AND FINAL VOLUME in Sanchez's Rainbow Boys trilogy finds the boys, Jason, Kyle, and Nelson, on a road trip from Washington, DC, to Los Angeles, where Jason—who lost a basketball scholarship when he came out—has been invited to speak at the opening of an alternative high school. Bisexual Jason and totally gay

Kyle are a couple (though perhaps questioning their relationship). Will pink-haired, flamboyant Nelson feel like a third wheel or will he find true love at long last? Their road trip offers a veritable real-life encyclopedia of the gay experience, as the three encounter a Britney Spears–lookalike transgender boy, a clutch of Radical Faeries who live off the land in rural Tennessee, a devoted gay couple who have been together for twenty years, and alas, the usual dangerous homophobes. Though a tad didactic, the novel nevertheless tells a compelling story and the characterization is well wrought, especially in the novel's second half. Fans of the Rainbow Boys won't want to miss this final installment of their adventures. **GA, QC**

Sanchez, Alex

So Hard to Say

Simon & Schuster, 2004. 240 p. ISBN: 9781416911890

CAN A BOY AND GIRL be just friends? That's the question that nags shy eighth grader Frederick, newly arrived in California, when he meets Xio and she develops a major crush on him. The problem is that Frederick is attracted to Victor, the captain of the school's soccer team. Does that mean he's gay? And what about Iggy, widely regarded as being gay and thus the subject of ridicule? Well, it's so hard to say. Searching for answers, the author tells his story from Frederick and Xio's alternating points of view. While Frederick as a character tends toward the stereotypical—he's asthmatic, is interested in interior decoration, is a neat freak, and so on—the story provides an intriguing examination of the evolving emotional lives of the two young teens. More important, this is one of the very few books with LGBTQ content featuring and published for middle school students. **HV, GA**

Schmatz, Pat
Mousetraps
Carolrhoda Books, 2008. 192 p. ISBN: 9780822586579

WHEN RICK, A FRIEND FROM childhood, enrolls in her school, Maxie rekindles her friendship with him. But it's complicated. Rick, who is thought to be gay, is a pariah, and Maxie still feels guilty for having abandoned him in seventh grade when a spiteful girl called her a fag hag. But is Rick gay, and how does he really feel about Maxie, and for that matter, how does she feel about him? Will history repeat itself? Meanwhile Maxie's favorite cousin, Sean, to whom she turns for counsel and comfort, is gay and in a loving relationship with high school football star Dex. It's noteworthy that Dex is African-American because people of color are a rarity in LGBTQ literature. It's also noteworthy that Sean's uncle, who has raised him, is also gay and in a relationship. Some of this seems improbable but is generally well handled and, happily, the characters invite readers' interest and sympathy. **HV, GA**

Selvadurai, Shyam
Swimming in the Monsoon Sea
Tundra, 2005. 224 p. ISBN: 9780887767357

THE YEAR IS 1980, the place is Sri Lanka, and fourteen-year-old Amrith is sick of the past. His parents died under mysterious circumstances when he was six. Since that time he has lived with his mother's best friend, Aunty Bundle, her husband Uncle Lucky, and their two daughters, Selvi and Mala. Then an uncle he has never known comes to Sri Lanka on business, bringing his sixteen-year-old son, Niresh. The two boys quickly become friends. For Amrith, however, the relationship is more than friendship, and he falls in love. Niresh, unaware of the depth of his cousin's feelings, begins showing tender feelings for Mala, which drives Amrith into a jealous rage. The theme of jealousy is underscored by the fact that Amrith has been selected to play the part of Desdemona in a school production of Othello (in his all-male school, female parts are played by boys). Amrith's unalloyed jealousy drives him and Niresh apart, but Amrith finally discovers that there is healing as well as pain in the past, and the two boys reconcile on the eve of Niresh's return to Canada. Amrith is left with the newfound knowledge that he is gay and hopes that someday he will find someone with whom to share this knowledge and, perhaps, his life. Selvadurai's coming-of-age novel is beautifully written, especially in its careful attention to the details of its lushly tropical setting. The characters are also drawn with care and psychological acuity, and the story is compelling and emotionally engaging. *Swimming in the Monsoon Sea* is an altogether remarkable work highly recommended for teens looking for literary fiction. **HV**

Singer, Marilyn

The Course of True Love Never Did Run Smooth

Harper & Row, 1983. 246 p. ISBN: 9780060257538

SIXTEEN-YEAR-OLD BECKY AND HER LONGTIME best friend, Nemi, (short for Nehemiah) have landed substantial parts in their Brooklyn, New York, high school production of *A Midsummer Night's Dream*. The play is both setting and sentiment in a story that begins with tryouts and ends with the players basking in the afterglow of a successful opening night. This novel does a fine job of capturing the intensity of a high school stage production as drama club regulars and first-timers bring their considerable energies together to create a classic story of star-crossed lovers enacted by teens who become star-crossed lovers themselves. As the show progresses it becomes increasingly clear that Becky and Nemi's friendship has turned to romantic love, and other romantic pairs start to emerge among the cast, including a same-sex couple, Richie (Demetrius) and Craig (Oberon), two boys whose mutual attraction is noted and accepted by their friends. There are various "true loves" in this novel, and though none of their paths run smooth, all are confident that their love is right for them. This is one of the first successful portrayals of gay assimilation in young adult fiction, as both same- and opposite-sex partners are simply part of New York City's cultural melting pot. **HV, GA**

Sloan, Brian

A Really Nice Prom Mess

Simon & Schuster, 2008. 320 p. ISBN: 9781416953890

TALK ABOUT A MESS! Sloan's first young adult novel is a fast-paced farce in which boyfriends Cameron and Shane decide to go to the prom together but with girls as their official "dates" so no one will find out they're gay. Unfortunately Cameron's

date, hot-tempered, red-haired Virginia quickly figures out that he is—gay, that is—and proceeds to get drunk as a sailor on shore leave, throwing up in a fish tank at a pre-prom party. Once at the dance Cameron and Shane get into an argument that results in blows and Cameron's leaving the dance with a Russian drug dealer/waiter he's met in the restroom. Before the evening is out, Cameron also will have met a deaf male stripper, a football player, and a sympathetic gay cop. Morning finds Cameron sadder but wiser about the capricious ways of the world and the unexpected perils of prom-going. Sloan is a filmmaker with a keen sense of the absurd, and it shows in the cinematic scene building and wacky encounters that distinguish the book. One of the too-rare comedic takes on the gay experience. **HV**

Sloan, Brian
Tale of Two Summers
Simon & Schuster, 2008. 245 p. ISBN: 9780689874390

WITH THE PROSPECT OF SPENDING their first summer apart, lifelong best friends Chuck and Hal decide to keep in touch by maintaining a blog. Accordingly the subsequent novel is told in their blog entries. For both boys summer is a time for love. Hal, who is gay, falls hard for French exchange student Henri. Chuck, who is straight, is equally smitten with Ghaliyah, a young woman from Saudi Arabia, who is Chuck's costar

Tale of Two Summers
Brian Sloan

in their summer drama camp production of Stephen Sondheim's *Merrily We Roll Along*. Thus, Chuck's blog entries chart the progress of the play's production as well as the progress—or lack thereof—of his infatuation with his costar. Hal has stayed at home, and his entries focus not only on the handsome Henri but also on his often humorous experiences in driving school. This tale gives thoughtful attention to both gay and straight relationships. As a result the pace of the early part of the novel is a bit slow, not unlike Chuck's description of *Merrily*: "It was kinda dull at first, because there was just so much damn talking." However, as the reader comes to know the two boys and as their relationships—including their friendship—become more complex, the plot becomes richer and the pace quickens dramatically. There is some explicit talk of sex—Chuck asks Hal what gays do in bed, for example—but, happily, none of it is gratuitous. **GA**

Smith, Andrew

Stick

Feiwel and Friends, 2011. 304 p. ISBN: 9780312613419

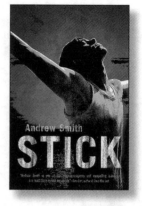

STICK, SO-CALLED BECAUSE at thirteen he is unusually tall and thin, was born with only one ear, which means he sometimes hears things differently, a fact reflected in his odd, occasionally truncated way of telling readers his story. ("I am so sorry." Overboard. And drowning.) He idolizes his older brother, Bosten, who Stick describes as "wild and rebellious like a horse that would rather die than submit to being ridden." Both boys are being physically abused by their thoroughly vile parents. As the story unfolds, it becomes clear that Bosten is also being sexually abused by their father. When the father discovers that Bosten is gay, there is a terrible fight and Bosten leaves home, destination unknown. Devastated, Stick "borrows" one of the family's two cars and sets off in pursuit of his brother. He heads for their great-aunt's house in Oxnard, California, where the brothers once spent an idyllic week, and there receives a phone call from Bosten telling him he is in Los Angeles. Stick heads to LA and discovers his brother is living on the street and abusing drugs. Can he persuade Bosten to return to Oxnard with him? Despite its evident darkness, *Stick* is a singularly gorgeous novel, made so by the brothers' love for each other and by Stick's realization of his love for his neighbor Emily. This is a beautifully realized, emotionally satisfying novel that evokes the work of both Adam Rapp (*33 Snowfish*) and Stephen Chbosky (*The Perks of Being a Wallflower*). And that is meant as high praise indeed. Another novel that is highly recommended. **GA**

Steinhofel, Andreas

The Center of the World

Delacorte Press, 2008. 480 p. ISBN: 9780307482716

SEVENTEEN-YEAR-OLD PHIL is an American living with his mother and twin sister, Dianne, in an ancient castle on the outskirts of a small, provincial German town, where all are definitely outsiders to the townspeople. Glass, their admittedly promiscuous mother, is regarded by the locals as a whore, and the twins as "the witch's children." Phil, who is gay, longs for intimacy and falls deeply in love with handsome runner Nicholas, who has taken the initiative in a steamy sexual relationship that is conducted silently and without emotional engagement. But when Phil introduces his friend

Katja, the mayor's daughter, to Nicholas, he invites a heartbreaking betrayal. In the meantime Phil is fascinated by his absent father, who lives in America, and by his own past. Accordingly the book is filled with flashbacks, which some readers will feel retard the action. Nevertheless, the book is beautifully written and careful readers will discover that it is, in many respects, a sophisticated contemporary fairy tale that rewards close reading. This novel received several prestigious awards in its native Germany and would be an excellent choice for teen readers who enjoy literary fiction. **GA**

Stevenson, Robin
Big Guy
Orca, 2008. 106 p. ISBN: 9781551439105

DEREK IS IN LOVE WITH Ethan whom he has only met online. Ethan reciprocates the emotion and excitedly reports that he will be coming to Ontario from British Columbia so the two can meet in person. But there is a problem: the picture Derek has sent him is an old one; since the photo was taken, he has gained eighty pounds, and Derek is afraid Ethan will reject him when he finds out. Meanwhile Derek has taken a job at a home for the elderly and disabled where he meets Aaliyah, a young woman who is similarly fearful about her relationship with her ex fiance. Together the two find the courage to pursue their hearts' desires. Stevenson manages to pack a lot of plot into a very brief book, a volume in Orca's Soundings series of hi-lo novels. Nevertheless, the characters are well and sympathetically developed and the plot is an engaging one with a satisfying and plausible denouement. **HV**

Sutherland, Suzanne
When We Were Good
Sumach Press, 2013. 227 p. ISBN: 9781927513118

THE 2000 Y2K SCARE IS now only a memory, but the panic it generated (many believed the shift from 1999 to 2000 would permanently crash the world's computers) remains real. The author makes the most of this setting in the coming-of-age story of Katherine Boatman, a Toronto teen whose personal world crashed on that fateful New Year's Eve. Katherine's ultra-successful parents (a popular television news anchor and a powerful international lawyer) have been largely absent, and she has been raised by her loving grandmother. When the grandmother suddenly collapses at the Boatmans' New Year's Eve party, she is whisked away and dies in the hospital. Katherine is shattered. Her grief and despair seem endless until she finds her grief unexpectedly eased by the painful honesty she hears in punk music. Her growing passion for punk draws her toward Marie, a like-minded and loquacious lesbian schoolmate. Their shared enthusiasm pulls them toward the live punk music scene. Although that particular scene is over, this narrative throws the reader back in time and makes the era live in the lyrics and the fans who find kindred spirits and healing through the timeless raw emotion of the music. **HV, GA, QC**

Taylor, William
The Blue Lawn
Alyson, 1999. 128 p. ISBN: 9781555834937

SET IN NEW ZEALAND, this is the story of fifteen-year-old David, a star rugby player who is strongly attracted to Theo, a new boy in his school. The slightly older Theo is living with his wealthy grandmother while his mother is abroad for a year. David soon learns that Theo is similarly drawn to him. Unexpectedly, a car crash provides the evidence when Theo wrecks his car while the two are on a drive in the country. Neither boy is hurt and, giddy with relief, Theo covers David's hand with his own. No words are exchanged, but both boys understand that their friendship might be more complex than they had thought. David is comfortable with this, but Theo is deeply conflicted about his feelings. "See," he later tells David, "I don't want to live with the idea that I'm a queer and that I'll always feel like this." Despite Theo's fears, their friendship grows and deepens, but Theo's grandmother grows increasingly suspicious of their closeness and effectively separates the two. However, it is clear that David's confidence in the rightness of their love is unshaken by her ignorant act. The writing effectively conveys both the pain and the magic of first love. **HV**

Volponi, Paul
Crossing Lines
Viking, 2011. 241 p. ISBN: 9780670012145

EFFEMINATE ALAN, THE NEW BOY in school, is widely regarded as being gay, a notion that is reinforced when he starts wearing lipstick and dresses to school.

Adonis, a member of the football team, at first goes along with the crowd, but when Alan befriends his younger sister, Adonis begins reexamining his stereotypical thinking, though he remains terrified that his teammates will think he is gay if he shows any sympathy for Alan—or Alana as he chooses to call himself. When Adonis's team loses its first game of the season, the players illogically blame Alan and vow to seek revenge by publicly humiliating him. When the plan goes terribly wrong, Adonis must choose how he will react. Will he continue to go along with the crowd, or will he finally choose to act as his conscience dictates? Although the plot is hardly original, Volponi's fast-paced story deftly examines stereotypical thinking and the kind of herd mentality that adolescents are prone to exhibit. Their too-easy assumption that Alan is gay is demonstrably wrong, but Volponi never reveals whether or not the boy is homosexual, though it's clear that Alan is in the process of coming to terms with being transgender. Compare this with Julie Anne Peters's *Luna* and Cris Beam's *I Am J.* **HV, GA**

Walker, Kate

Peter

Houghton Mifflin, 1993. 240 p. ISBN: 9780618111305

PETER, A FIFTEEN-YEAR-OLD AUSTRALIAN BOY, spends his days with his dirt-biking buddies in their endless competition to out-do each other in increasingly risky feats of derring-do. Peter's ultimate ambitions are simple: get a road license for his dirt bike, finish school, and find a job with cameras. But things begin to change when he meets David, his college-student brother's best friend. David is openly gay, and Peter begins to worry that the strong attraction he feels to the older boy may mean that he too is gay. For Peter, whose knowledge of homosexuality is rooted in societal stereotypes, the prospect is not pleasing: "I didn't want to be a poofter job, a social outcast, a candidate for AIDS." At the same time, it's clear that David is in fact a warm, intelligent, caring human being who provides Peter with a far more attractive model of maleness than his peers' macho posturing. This story follows Peter as he takes his first tentative steps toward the man he will become. **HV, GA**

Walker, Paul Robert

The Method

Gulliver/HBJ, 1990. 181 p. ISBN: 9780152012601

FIFTEEN-YEAR-OLD WOULD-BE ACTOR Albie joins an intensive summer workshop in method acting, where he meets and befriends another student, Mitch. He also learns that his drama teacher, Mr. Pierce, is gay. Later, when Mitch takes an unsuspecting Albie to that annual celebration of LGBTQ life, a gay pride parade, and then to a crowded gay restaurant, he comes out to Albie, who at first laughs in disbelief until Mitch explains, "I'm sorry that makes you nervous Albie. But I want you to know. I'm gay. I'm queer. I'm a faggot. I'm homosexual. This is not a joke. This is my life." When Mitch then asks if they're still friends, Albie's response is to cover Mitch's hand with his own and say, simply, "You know we are." Though the setting—the theater—is a conventional, almost stereotypical one for a gay novel, *The Method* is notable not only for Albie's heartwarming acceptance of his friend's homosexuality, but also for being the first to include a gay pride parade. Even more important, it demonstrates in the parade and the gay restaurant that homosexuals, who too often had been portrayed as unhappy loners, actually have a community of other gay people with whom they can mingle and socialize. Though not perfect—some of the characters and situations come dangerously close to being stereotypical—*The Method* nevertheless makes an important contribution to the evolving field of LGBTQ literature. **HV, QC**

Watts, Julia

Finding H.F.

Alyson Publications, 2001. 165 p. ISBN: 9781594932854

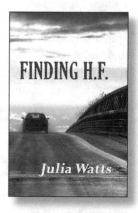

ABANDONED AS AN INFANT by her fifteen-year-old mother, H.F. (Heavenly Faith) is raised in Morgan, Kentucky, by her loving and very religious grandmother, Memaw. As an illegitimate tomboy with a growing attraction to women, H.F.'s sense of difference has been lifelong, and her first-person narrative voice is fresh, intelligent, and wryly self-aware. Her best friend, Bo, a self-described "sissy-boy," shares her sense of alienation. Both of these gender nonconformists are well aware of their deviance from the norms of their community, yet both are managing to struggle through adolescence toward an adulthood where they can spread their wings and find the larger lives they imagine for themselves. Just when H.F. is rejected by the girl of her dreams, she finds the address of the mother she's never known and persuades Bo to drive with her to Florida in search of her. As they make their way from Kentucky to Florida they meet three homeless lesbian teens, visit a gay bookstore, attend a gay-friendly church service, and experience the thrill of seeing two men casually walking hand in hand through a public park. In short, they gain a vision of the post–high school world that awaits them: not a utopia by any means, but one that has ample room for them and all those other "people like us." **HV, GA, QC**

Wilkinson, Lili
Pink
HarperTeen, 2009. 310 p. ISBN: 9780061926532

IS IT POSSIBLE TO BOTH fit in *and* be yourself? This Australian import tells the story of sixteen-year-old Ava, who's exploring this question. As a young girl, Ava was all pink all the time—pink dresses, pink bedroom walls, even pink pencils—but in the years since then she's come to see pink as "an empty signifier of femininity" and has become a self-described "quasi-goth emo lesbian." But who is she really? Well, she *knows* she wants to go to university after high school, so she applies to an academically rigorous private high school, sheds her black clothing in favor of a new look—a pink cashmere sweater!—and considers looking for a boyfriend. She enjoys the intellectual challenge of her new classes in a school where "being smart wasn't considered a sign of mental instability," but is this a place where she can fit in? Can she tell her new friends she's a lesbian? Can she tell her old friends that she's wearing pink? How long can she keep her various worlds from colliding? And where—and who—will she be when they do? Witty dialog and just the right blend of naïveté and snarkiness describe Ava's search for identity and kindred spirits. **HV, GA**

Wilson, Martin
What They Always Tell Us
Delacorte Press, 2008. 304 p. ISBN: 9780385735070

SINCE ALEX DRANK PINE-SOL in a vain attempt at suicide, he has been a pariah. Even his older brother, James, is uncomfortable around him. But then Nathen, one of James's friends, befriends Alex and things begin to change . . . for the better.

Readers are sure to fall in love with these wonderful characters, applaud the growing closeness between the two brothers, and admire the beautifully realized love relationship between Alex and Nathen. A subplot involving Henry, the lonely little boy across the street who may make readers think of a younger Alex, adds texture to this already rich novel. In his superb first book, Wilson demonstrates a wonderful gift for finding the truth in human caring and for creating memorably multidimensional and engagingly sympathetic characters whom readers will welcome into their hearts. This is clearly one of the best LGBTQ novels of the past decade and a superb work of fiction in any category. **HV**

Wittlinger, Ellen
Hard Love
Simon & Schuster, 1999. 224 p. ISBN: 9780689841545

A PRINTZ HONOR AWARD BOOK and groundbreaking novel, this is a story set in Boston and told by John "Gio" Galardi, a "hollow soul trying to pass for normal," who meets Marisol Guzman, a self-proclaimed "Puerto Rican Cuban Yankee Lesbian." The two connect through both their mutual appreciation for each other's zines—John's *Bananafish* and Marisol's *Escape Velocity*—and their distrust of adult/parental hypocrisy even as they themselves are moving toward adulthood. John's relationship with his divorced parents is especially painful, and he's responded to their unavailability by distancing himself mentally and emotionally from everyone in his life. John and Marisol are kindred spirits, but as their friendship develops, John finds himself falling in love with the prickly and charismatic Marisol. Over the years there have been a number of YA novels featuring a young woman's impossible attraction to a gay man, but this is the first YA novel to explore the same painful longing from the perspective of a young man's feelings of attraction to a lesbian woman. **GA, QC**

Wittlinger, Ellen
Heart on My Sleeve
Simon & Schuster, 2004. 219 p. ISBN: 9780689849992

TOLD IN THE FORM OF e-mails, IMs, and snail mail, Wittlinger's novel charts the summer romance of Chloe and Julian, who meet at their college's summer orientation weekend for entering students. The two bond and begin e-mailing each other and gradually falling in love. In the meantime Chloe's older sister, Genevieve, has also fallen in love—with another girl, Alice. When Genevieve comes out to her sister in an e-mail, Chloe reacts with anger and sorrow—anger that her sister has kept such a major part of her life a secret and sorrow that Genevieve will never have a husband and children. Genevieve's parents react badly too, finding the news "shocking" and deploring what they describe as their daughter's new "lifestyle." They further betray their ignorance by blaming their daughter's homosexuality on her acting career "and the kind of people one associates with in that type of business." They even benightedly wonder if this is a stage that Genevieve is passing through as they contemplate the "strange, lonely life" she will lead. Will Chloe and the parents come to accept Genevieve's sexual identity? And what will happen with Chloe and Julian's summer romance, not to mention Genevieve and Alice's? The realistic answers are not necessarily all happy ones, but in each case, they leave the characters—and the readers—wiser in the ways of romance and love. **HV, QC**

Wittlinger, Ellen
Love & Lies: Marisol's Story
Simon & Schuster, 2008. 245 p. ISBN: 9781416962311

AUTHOR WITTLINGER CONTINUES THE STORY begun in her Printz Honor–title *Hard Love*. Aspiring author Marisol has deferred college for a year to write a novel. Hoping to hone her skills, she enrolls in a community college writing class where she immediately falls in love with Olivia, her beautiful, charismatic teacher. Meanwhile she has met Lee, a newcomer who has moved to Massachusetts from Indiana, and the two become friends—and maybe more; it's clear that Lee has a crush on her. As her relationship with Olivia heats up, Marisol discovers that Olivia is not quite what she seems. Love and lies become tangled, and soon Marisol isn't sure what the truth is. Fortunately she has her gay roommates, Birdie and Damon, and her straight friend, Gio (also from *Hard Love*), to help her find the truth in love. But is it too late? Wittlinger has written another sensitive and wise coming-of-age novel that will appeal to gay teens and enlighten straight ones. **GA**

Wittlinger, Ellen
Parrotfish
Simon & Schuster, 2007. 304 p. ISBN: 9781442406216

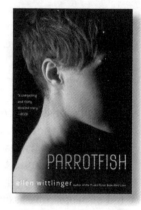

SOCIETY LIKES TO LABEL PEOPLE, and Angela McNair has been labeled as having "gender dysphoria." What this means in human terms is that Angela occupies the wrong body. Born a girl, she knows that she is really a boy. And so she bravely begins transforming herself into a male. She cuts her hair short, buys men's clothing, and announces that her name is now "Grady." And, oh yes, she falls in love with Kita, a mixed-race girl. Grady's transition—though bold—is surprisingly easy; he finds loving support from his family and from a female gym teacher at school. This is not to say he doesn't encounter some hostility, but no blood is shed nor is his life threatened. Some readers, in fact, may find his transition too easy, but there is no question that Wittlinger does a superb job of untangling the complexities of gender identity and producing a reasoned approach to a—for its time—controversial, hot-button issue. Most important, this is a groundbreaking work, only the second novel to feature a transgender teen. The first, of course, was Julie Anne Peters's *Luna*. Both are essential reading. **GA**

Wittlinger, Ellen
What's in a Name?
Simon & Schuster, 2000. 146 p. ISBN: 9781416984825

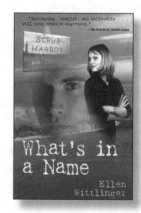

FIFTEEN-YEAR-OLD O'NEILL'S class assignment sounds simple: write a poem that answers the question, Who am I? To write it, his English teacher, Mr. Tompkins, glibly says, "Spend one whole day being totally honest with yourself and everybody else." Simple? Not for O'Neill, who has kept his gayness a closely guarded secret. He can be honest with himself but is he really ready to out himself to others? "Can't I hide a while longer?" he thinks wistfully. The question of course is, Will he come out? And if he does, what impact will it have on his football star older brother and on the girl who has a crush on him? Readers will find out in Wittlinger's collection of ten linked stories about identity, about coming to terms with yourself, and about telling the truth. O'Neill addresses this when he speaks to his school's Gay-Straight Alliance: "Then one day it just hit me that I didn't have any friends . . . because I was a liar. So I'm tired of lying to myself or anybody else. I'm gay. I don't expect everybody to like me all of a sudden. But at least now whether you like me or not, you'll know who I am." Readers will too. **HV, GA, QC**

Woodson, Jacqueline
After Tupac and D Foster
Putnam, 2008. 153 p. ISBN: 9780399246548

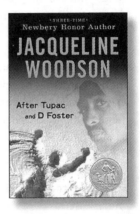

D. (FOR DESIREE) IS A ROAMER, searching for her Big Purpose. En route she meets the unnamed narrator and her best friend, Neeka, and the three girls bond, united in part by their love for Tupac Shakur and his music. Their only reservation is the way he and other rappers dis homosexuals, since Neeka's oldest brother, Tash, is gay and a queen or, as the narrator candidly puts it, "a true-blue sissy (who) wasn't afraid to let the world know it." Tash is comfortable with himself, but not everybody else is. When his family visits him in jail (he's imprisoned for allegedly participating in a violent crime) and his mother tries to discourage him from being flamboyant around his younger siblings, he says—movingly—"Mama, I'm in jail. Give me a little bit of joy. I ain't hurting nobody. I ain't *never* tried to hurt nobody who wasn't hurting me first. I know who I am and you know who I am and every one of these kids knows who I am. Ain't that good enough . . . Ain't I good enough?" Though Tash is only a secondary character, he is a large presence in this novel about injustice and identity. It is the enigmatic D., however, who is the major presence in the lives of Neeka and the narrator. And the possibility that she may leave them when she is reunited with her mother is a cause for consternation and the possibility of heartbreak, which is what the girls actually experience when Tupac is murdered. Is D. also gone forever? Not all the parts of Woodson's multifaceted novel cohere, but its overall tone is consistent in its haunting treatment of friendship and love, found and lost. **GA**

Woodson, Jacqueline

From the Notebooks of Melanin Sun

Scholastic, 1995. 176 p. ISBN: 9780142416419

THIRTEEN-YEAR-OLD MELANIN SUN, an African-American teen with a talent for writing, lives in Brooklyn, New York, with his single mother, EC. Mel and EC have been a tight-knit family of two for as long as he can remember, and they are having an ordinary summer: EC is working and going to school while Mel spends his days hanging out with his friends Ralph and Sean—and crushing out on a neighborhood girl and classmate, Angie. But their ordinary summer suddenly changes when EC tells him "someone special" is coming for dinner, and that someone turns out to be a white woman named Kristen. The next week EC tells him she's in love with Kristen. He reacts with anger and something close to panic. How could his mother fall in love with a woman? And, more important, does his mother's love for a woman mean that she will stop loving him? He worries that Kristen's regular presence in their neighborhood will alienate Ralph and Sean, not to mention Angie. Mel and his friends routinely dis "faggots" and "dykes," but if they find out that EC is gay, will they think that he is gay too? Will they still be his friends? Mel tells the story of the summer that rocked his world in two voices as he alternately addresses the reader in the text and himself in his ever-present notebook. Mel's story is a compelling one. **HV, QC**

Woodson, Jacqueline

The House You Pass on the Way

Scholastic, 1997. 112 p. ISBN: 9780142417065

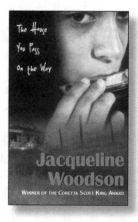

SELF-NAMED STAGGERLEE CANAN is the child of a white mother and an African-American father living in the rural South. Her father is the son of two larger-than-life civil rights movement heroes martyred by a bomb set off at a civil rights demonstration in the years before her parents married. Staggerlee is the middle child of five, a quiet loner who keeps her own counsel. She is close to her parents and older brother but isolated from her peers and wonders if she will ever have a friend. Racism on both sides of the family has long isolated the Canans from any experience of extended family, but this changes when Staggerlee's beautiful cousin

Trout, another self-named fourteen-year-old, comes to stay for the summer. Both Staggerlee and Trout find a kindred spirit in each other; their connection grows and deepens throughout Trout's visit yet remains ambiguous. As they write in the riverbank mud, "Staggerlee and Trout were here today. Maybe they will and maybe they won't be gay." **HV**

Wolff, Virginia Euwer
True Believer
Atheneum, 2001. 264 p. ISBN: 9780689852886

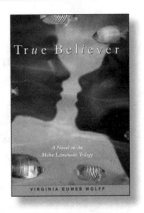

THE SECOND BOOK IN THE author's Make Lemonade trilogy of verse novels is again narrated by LaVaughn, a fifteen-year-old working-class girl whose life has begun to change around her. Her longtime best friends, Myrtle and Annie, are urging her to join their Cross Your Legs for Jesus Club. Her mother is entertaining her first serious suitor since the death of LaVaughn's father. And she encounters her childhood pal Jody, who has moved into her building and become "too gorgeous to look at head on." LaVaughn is also changing ("my hope is strong like an athlete") as she pursues her future goal of college. She's enrolled in advanced college-readiness courses, and her new classmates share her ambitions, as does Jody, whose swim team success may be his ticket to higher education. He greets LaVaughan with a ready smile and attends a school dance with her, but it's clear to the reader that her hoped-for romance is a non-starter. Her aggrieved astonishment at seeing him kiss another boy is real, as is her pain at losing a might-have-been dream of romance. But LaVaughan's hope carries her through in this beautifully written novel. **HV**

Wright, Bil
Putting Makeup on the Fat Boy
Simon & Schuster, 2011. 240 p. ISBN: 9781416939962

HIGH SCHOOL STUDENT CARLOS secures a part-time job at Macy's cosmetics counter and dreams of a career as make-up artist to the stars. Be careful what you wish for because—believe it or not—a genuine star comes into the store and is instantly taken with Carlos's abilities. Comic complications ensue. As if Carlos doesn't have enough troubles—he is also struggling with his boss's antagonism and his sister's Neanderthal boyfriend's homophobic verbal abuse. And did I also mention that Carlos has a serious crush on Gleason, a cute boy at school? Yes, Wright (*Sunday You Learn How to Box*, below) manages to pack a lot of plot into 240 pages. But it's all done artfully and with good humor. Carlos is definitely a keeper and is one of the few Latino protagonists of an LGBTQ novel. The book is winner of a 2012 Stonewall Book Award. **GA**

Wright, Bil
Sunday You Learn How to Box
Simon & Schuster, 2000. 218 p. ISBN: 9781442474727

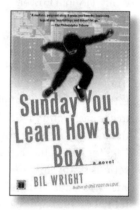

SET IN CONNECTICUT'S STRATFIELD PROJECTS in 1968, Wright's accomplished first novel is the story of fourteen-year-old Louis Bowman. The boy's emerging homosexuality makes him an easy target for the project's bullies, so his mother, Jeanette, persuades his antagonistic stepfather, Ben, to give him boxing lessons each Sunday. Unfortunately the "lessons" quickly turn into weekly sessions of battering and physical abuse. Louis's grades begin to drop and he is diagnosed with depression. What keeps him whole is his crush on an older boy, Ray Anthony Robinson, whom the neighbors dismiss as a hoodlum. Though nothing comes of the crush except a kind of distant friendship, the emotions it generates in young Louis are a beacon of light in his otherwise dark existence. To Wright's credit, he depicts the boy's budding homosexuality not as cause for self-hatred and despair but instead as a positive force in his life. *Sunday You Learn How to Box* is an important contribution to LGBT literature not only because it is a fine stand-alone novel, but also because it is one of only a handful of LGBT novels to feature a protagonist of color (see also Wright's *Putting Makeup on the Fat Boy*, above). **HV**

Wyeth, Sharon Dennis
Orphea Proud
Delacorte Press, 2004. 208 p. ISBN: 9780385324977

ORPHANED AT AGE EIGHT, ORPHEA is living with her strict half-brother and his wife. Now sixteen, she realizes she is in love with her longtime best friend, Lissa. When the half-brother discovers the two in bed together, he strikes Orphea, and the terrified Lissa flees and is killed in a car crash. Devastated, Orphea is then sent to

live with her elderly great-aunts in rural Virginia. There she finds the loving support and acceptance that have been missing from her life. The book's conceit is that the story is all part of a performance piece—including poetry—that Orphea is presenting at a club in Queens, New York. Realistically speaking, the piece is probably too long for actual presentation, and the car crash death of a gay teen is an ancient and outmoded trope in LGBT literature. That said, the story is heartfelt and affecting and the fact that its protagonist is African-American—a rarity in LGBTQ fiction—recommend it for consideration. **HV**

Yamanaka, Lois-Ann
Name Me Nobody
Hyperion, 1999. 229 p. ISBN: 9780786814664

SET IN HAWAII, THIS IS the story of Emi-Lou Kaya's fourteenth summer, which she spends—as always—following the lead of her best friend Yvonne ("Where Von goes, Emi-Lou goes"). The two have been inseparable since childhood. At age nine they pressed their pricked fingers together: "'Us against the world,' Von said. . . . 'We will always be together.'" Yvonne is tall and athletic, a valued member of her softball team. Emi is short and clumsy but fiercely determined to stay close to Von. Emi succeeds in joining the team, but then Von discovers women, and Emi is at a loss. Specifically, Von becomes involved with Babes, another softball team member, and Von's time with Emi shrinks accordingly. Emi is resentful of Babes and treats her scornfully, for there is no place for her feelings of anger and loss in the growing attraction between Von and Babes. How much trouble can Emi make for the two girls before Von's parents learn the truth about their daughter's relationship with Babes? And what will happen when they do? Emi tells her story in colloquial Hawaiian Creole English, which gives the narrative a flavor unusual in books for teen readers—this isn't dialect, there is no phonetic spelling, but the dialog has a realistic lilt that is, unfortunately, rare in books for teen readers. **HV**

Yee, Paul
Money Boy
Groundwood, 2011. 192 p. ISBN: 9781554980949

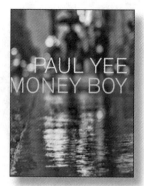

WHEN CHINESE-CANADIAN IMMIGRANT RAY'S militaristic father discovers he is gay, he kicks him out of the house. A child of privilege, Ray is completely at sea and is soon mugged and his wallet and ID are stolen. For a while it appears he may have to become a "money boy," prostituting himself to survive, but fortunately before that can happen, he discovers a supportive gay community to help him. Set in Toronto, which boasts Canada's largest Chinese population, *Money Boy* is noteworthy as being one of the very few LGBTQ novels to feature an Asian protagonist. **HV, QC**

Graphic Novels

nce dismissed as "mere comics," graphic novels (GNs) have come of age as a form of sequential visual art that is now taken seriously (and deservedly so!). The GNs that follow are among the best of this rapidly growing universe of titles. In selecting them we applied the same criteria to the same narrative elements (plot, characters, setting, theme, language, etc.) that we used in evaluating the fiction titles that precede them. We also looked for originality and for LGBTQ content that avoids two-dimensional LGBTQ stereotypes in favor of fully realized characters and situations. And finally, we evaluated the art that accompanies the text of each and considered the harmony between the two elements. For example, does the art simply illustrate the text, or does it enhance and expand the overall narrative? Graphic novels, as you will see, include a variety of different genres. The titles below include humor, coming-of-age, action adventure, fantasy, romance, and mystery. And, despite the fact that "novel" commonly refers to a work of fiction, the world of GNs includes true stories, so you'll also find nonfiction, including biography and autobiography. In addition to our descriptive annotations, we also include the codes (HV, GA, QC) used in the Fiction section (see pages 1–2). We hope you'll enjoy the annotations that follow.

Books

Bechdel, Alison
Fun Home: A Family Tragicomic
Houghton Mifflin, 2006. 240 p. ISBN: 9780618871711

THIS CELEBRATED MEMOIR BY BECHDEL (*Dykes to Watch Out For*) is a marvel of art and integrity. Smart and insightful, it is the story of her childhood growing up in a small Pennsylvania town where her father worked as both a high school English teacher and mortician. As children, Bechdel and her siblings refer to the Bechdel Funeral Home as the "fun home," hence the title. Aside from the author/artist herself, the principal player in her life is her father, a reserved, emotionally cold man whose passion is restoring the family's Victorian-era house, a project that involves the entire family and a spate of teenage boys. As Bechdel grows up, she begins to realize that she is a lesbian. It's when she comes out that she learns her father is himself a closeted homosexual and has had relationships with his students and the children's male babysitter. Shortly after Bechdel learns her father's secret, he is killed in an accident that was most probably a suicide. That Bechdel shared not only a sexual identity but also a literary sensibility with her father adds another layer of thematic meaning to this exceptionally rich and psychologically complex graphic novel, which has been compared to Proust and Joyce. It is a winner of the prestigious Eisner Award. **HV, QC**

Braddock, Paige
Jane's World Collection
Girl Twirl Comics, 2007. 432 p. ISBN: 9780976670780

THIS COLLECTION CONTAINS THE FIRST three volumes of Braddock's Eisner-nominated comic, which stars Jane Tiberius (her father was a *Star Trek* fan!) Wyatt, a young lesbian who lives in a trailer with her straight (male) friend Ethan. Other recurring characters include Sarah, Jane's ex girlfriend; Becca, Jane's sister; and Chelle, Jane's occasional bête noire and sometime girlfriend. Jane has a variety of adventures, some of them fantastic (she is abducted by aliens, she is washed up on an island of Amazons, her hamster hires a lawyer) and others, more realistic (she gets fired from her job at a newspaper, goes to work at a convenience store, breaks up with her girlfriend). The tone is light, quirky, often whimsical, and regularly funny. Launched in 1998, the strip became the first gay-themed comic to be distributed by a national media syndicate. **GA**

Cruse, Howard
Stuck Rubber Baby
Foreword by Alison Bechdel. Vertigo, 2010. 224 p.
ISBN: 9781401227135 (original edition: Stuck Rubber
Baby. Introduction by Tony Kushner. DC Comics, 2000.
216 p. ISBN: 9781563892554)

FIRST PUBLISHED IN 1995 by Paradox Press (an imprint of DC), this is a classic among graphic novels. Semiautobiographical, it is the story of a young white working-class man, Toland Polk, who is coming of age in the South during the civil rights era and struggling—not always successfully—to come to terms with his homosexuality. The extremely complex story is told in retrospect by an adult Toland recalling the events that changed his life, including a doomed romance with a female friend, his involvement in the civil rights movement, and his participation in the black community, which includes a brief affair with a black man. In an interview Cruse stated, "My goal was to create the kind of novel that is too full of incident for someone to simply summarize in their mind in one sentence." He has succeeded; indeed his art, using a detailed cross-hatching technique, is as dense as the story. In a thoughtful introduction playwright Tony Kushner calls Cruse "a pioneer in the field of lesbian and gay comics, an important participant in the underground comics movement, and in my opinion one of the most talented artists ever to work in the form." The most recent (2010) edition includes an introduction by the cartoonist and graphic novelist Alison Bechdel. **HV**

Denson, Abby
Tough Love: High School Confidential
Manic D. Press, 2006. 137 p. ISBN: 9781933149080

BRIAN AND CHRIS MEET AT their high school karate class and are instantly attracted to each other. In short order the two become boyfriends, though Chris is still recovering from the end of his relationship with Li, whose parents—upon discovering his homosexuality—send him to live with family in China. There, after sending Brian a suicide note, he slashes his wrists. Fortunately he recovers and, returning to the United States, attempts to resume his relationship with Chris. Will

Chris reciprocate? What will happen with Brian? Denson has created a sweet-spirited, occasionally suspenseful high school romance between two engaging boys. In addition to first love (Brian has never had a boyfriend), the author's plot line includes such familiar rite-of-passage experiences as coming out and dealing with homophobia, but their presentation is nevertheless fresh and appealing. The simple black-and-white drawings capture the mood and tone of the uncomplicated text, offering a good read for middle school students. **HV, GA**

Fish, Tim

Strugglers

Poison Press, 2006. 111 p. ISBN: 9780976278364

MEET THE STRUGGLERS: TRACEY AND Alison; their roommate, Tighe; and Mike, the boy next door. All of them are struggling in their individual ways: Tracey and Alison are both in rock bands striving for success, though in their personal lives it is Tracey who is ambitious while Alison is the consummate slacker. Tighe is struggling with his sexual identity, trying to come to terms with the fact that he is gay. Mike is comfortable with his own homosexuality, but his fraternity brothers may not be. The two boys are attracted to each other and, after some serious flirting, have a brief affair, but Tighe's uncertainties soon put an end to it, leaving Mike still looking for love. All the lead characters are appealing, though it is the boys who are the best developed and whose story, for gay readers, is the most engaging. The black-and-white art is serviceable but rough, and the appearance of the characters often changes, making it somewhat difficult for readers to identify them. However, the text is well done and the plot satisfying. A good read for older teens. **HV**

Hagio, Moto

The Heart of Thomas

Fantagraphics, 2012. 515 p. ISBN: 9781606995518

NOW PUBLISHED IN THE UNITED STATES for the first time, this is a classic example of shojo (girl's) manga and one of the first examples of *shonen-ai* (boy love

novels). Set in a German boarding school, it begins with the enigmatic death of fourteen-year-old Thomas, who leaves a note for another boy, Juli, declaring his love. The highly romantic story then follows the uneasy friendships of Juli, the rebellious Oskar, and a new transfer student, Erich, who looks exactly like Thomas. The complexities—and length—of the plot make it impossible to summarize; suffice it to say that, though published in Japan in 1974, it remains a classic and is offered here as a paradigmatic work of *shonen-ai*. **GA**

Kelly, David

Rainy Day Recess

Northwest Press, 2011. 119 p.
ISBN: 9780984594023

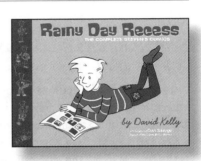

"STEVEN'S COMICS," ABOUT A SENSITIVE fourth-grade boy, ran in gay and alternative newspapers from 1995 to 1998. Set in the 1970s, the strip follows the daily life of the fourth grader and features such stories as Steven's crushes on his new best friend, Christopher, and on a high school boy, Troy, who is his swimming coach; on his getting a Wonder Woman doll (er, action figure!); on his wearing his sister's platform shoes (and twisting his ankle); and more. The book collects the entire series plus additional material created especially for this volume. The text-rich panels and cartoon black-and-white drawings evoke the style and spirit of Lynda Barry's expressionist art. Funny and sweet-spirited, *Rainy Day Recess* is a delight. **HV**

Merey, Ilike

a + e 4EVER

Lethe Press, 2011. 214 p. ISBN: 9781590213902

EULALIE AND ASHER ARE TALKING about sex: "So what do you call yourself," she asks him, "gay?" "I don't know," he answers, "why do I have to call it anything?" Why, indeed? As this fine graphic novel artfully demonstrates, sexual identity can be deeply ambiguous and appearances, deceiving. Asher, for example, is an artist who is beautifully androgynous and accordingly is widely perceived at school as being gay. Similarly, tall and tough-minded Eulalie is assumed to be a lesbian. While there is truth in these perceptions, it's not the whole truth. Asher may be better described as being bisexual, while Eu, as she's called, has affairs with boys. So what does that make them and what does it mean for their evolving friendship, which begins as platonic and gradually becomes something deeper? Author-artist Merey does an excellent job of making sense of these uncertainties, aided by the manga-inspired pen-and-ink drawings of various sizes that decorate each page and range from sketchy to lush, capturing and expanding the mood and tone of the text. The result is deeply affecting and emotionally engaging as the two appealing teens explore and define their sexuality. **HV**

O'Malley, Bryan Lee
Scott Pilgrim's Precious Little Life
Color ed. Oni Press, 2012. 191 p. ISBN: 9781620100004

THIS FIRST OF SIX VOLUMES introduces Scott Pilgrim, a twenty-three-year-old Canadian slacker who lives in Toronto with his gay roommate, the rather fabulous, witty, and wry Wallace. Currently unemployed, Scott is the bassist in a band that calls itself Sex Bob-omb. The other two band members are Stephen Stills, guitar (yes, he's named for the famous musician), and Kim Pine, drums. To the consternation of his friends, Scott has begun dating a seventeen-year-old high school student named Knives Chau. Since theirs is a chaste relationship—they haven't even kissed—Scott views it as blameless. Things get complicated, though, when our hero then meets the girl of his dreams (literally), Ramona Flowers. Scott finds himself in an epic—okay, *cosmic*—fight with the first of Ramona's evil exes, Matthew Patel, whom he defeats even though Patel has the supernatural power to summon "demon hipster chicks" to assist him. After the fight, Scott and Ramona agree to start dating, providing that he defeat her six other evil exes. Stay tuned . . . Made into a movie starring Michael Cera, *Scott Pilgrim* is a thoroughly delightful read that will have readers clamoring for succeeding volumes. **GA**

Parent, Dan
Archie's Pal Kevin Keller
Archie Comic Publications, 2012. Unpaged.
ISBN: 9781879794931

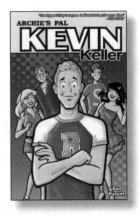

MEET KEVIN KELLER, THE NEWEST inhabitant of the Archie universe. When the introduction to this landmark volume says, "Archie is for EVERYONE!" it's not an overstatement because—in Kevin—Archie comics has its first openly gay character. "Kevin is the all-American teenager who just happens to be gay," the introduction asserts. And that's perhaps the best part about the new character: he's gay, but that doesn't completely define him. He's also funny, smart, and handsome, and he has an appetite as big as Jughead's—no mean feat! In this first of a series of adventures (nine additional volumes at last count), Kevin comes to Riverdale and casually comes out to Jughead. In the meantime Veronica, who doesn't know the truth, has fallen head over heels in love with him. When she finally learns he's gay, she and Kevin become BFFs, making Betty jealous. But everything is soon smoothed over and order is restored to Riverdale. The reader also learns about Kevin's childhood and family (he's an army brat), cheers him on as he wins the annual Witmaster competition, and rejoices when he's elected class president. The new kid in town, who just happens to be gay, has made good. **GA**

Road, Cristy C.
Spit and Passion
The Feminist, 2013. 128 p. ISBN: 9781558618077

THIS SEMIAUTOBIOGRAPHICAL COMING-OF-AGE graphic novel features the Cuban-American author at twelve as she deals with identity issues, including her emerging homosexuality. Growing up in a female-centric Catholic household, she is not yet out. "I liked to see my closet as a safe and alternate universe of us vs. them, and now vs. later." She finds comfort and inspiration in the music of the punk band Green Day ("The summer of 1994 . . . I listened to Green Day every day until my ears bled.") and in role models like Roseanne Barr and Ellen DeGeneres. The black-and-white art captures the occasionally angsty spirit of the text, though the latter sometimes overwhelms the former, at times turning this into more illustrated book than graphic novel. Readers may notice one amusing visual quirk: Road looks disconcertingly (intentionally?) like the Mexican artist Frida Kahlo. **HV**

Rucka, Greg and Michael Lark

Half a Life

DC Comics, 2003. 160 p. ISBN: 9781401204389

GOTHAM CITY POLICE DETECTIVE RENEE Montoya is being sued for ten million dollars by a former defendant named Marty Lipari, when she is unexpectedly outed (yes, she's a lesbian) by someone seeking revenge. Her deeply religious immigrant parents are devastated, and many of her colleagues on the force abandon her just when she needs support and understanding the most. Then Lipari is murdered and Renee is accused of the crime and arrested. The plot thickens significantly when a notorious criminal named Two Face becomes involved. Lark's noir art matches the dark tone of the text, and together they tell a compelling story of injustice and justice served. The lesbian content is extremely well handled, and the gritty atmosphere is tempered somewhat by the fact that Renee has a lover, a pastry chef named Daria. *Half a Life* won the prestigious Eisner Award for best story of the year. It also collected the Harvey, Eagle, and Prism Awards. It's an excellent addition to LGBTQ literature. **HV**

Schrag, Ariel

Awkward and Definition: The High School Comic Chronicles of Ariel Schrag

Touchstone, 2008. 144 p. ISBN: 9781416552314.

Potential

Touchstone, 2008. 232 p. ISBN: 9781416552352.

Likewise

Touchstone, 2009. 400 p. ISBN: 9781416552376.

BEGUN WHEN SHE WAS STILL a student at Berkeley (California) High School, these four volumes in three books chronicle the author/artist's high school years. Each volume is devoted to a single year, thus, *Awkward* covers her freshman year; *Definition*, her sophomore year; *Potential*, her junior year; and *Likewise*, her senior year. Originally self-published, the series was subsequently picked up by Slave Labor Graphics and, more recently, Touchstone. Distinguished by its frankness, the series chronicles the everyday experiences and angst of an unusually perspicacious teenager who is coming of age emotionally and physically. In *Potential* Schrag comes to terms with being a lesbian, and later episodes record moments from her love life. Some of this material has been controversial for its openness. Some of her scenes, reviewer Francisca Goldsmith notes in her *Booklist* review of *Potential*, "may outrage the straitlaced." Others will praise the same scenes for their authenticity and frankness. Teen readers have embraced Schrag's work, recognizing themselves in its depiction of the ups and downs of adolescent life. **GA**

Shanower, Eric

Age of Bronze: A Thousand Ships

Image Comics, 2001. 208 p. ISBN: 9781582402000.

See also **Age of Bronze: Sacrifice** *(ISBN: 9781582403601) and* **Age of Bronze: Betrayal, Part One** *(ISBN: 9781582408453).*

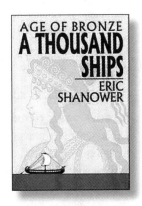

SHANOWER'S AGE OF BRONZE SERIES is a masterful and compelling retelling of the story of the Trojan War. Twice winner of the prestigious Eisner Award, the story will ultimately occupy nine volumes (at least that's Shanower's estimate at this time). As these first three volumes demonstrate, Shanower is a brilliant draftsman and his black-and-white art is nothing short of inspired. His text is equally superb, formal but never self-consciously ornate. It is obvious that his research is meticulous (as are his drawings), recreating the period and setting with authenticity and integrity. The homosexual content (e.g., the love story of Achilles and Patroklus) respects Homer's original telling and is beautifully and sensitively rendered. *Age of Bronze* is a modern masterpiece in the making. **GA**

Takako, Shimura. Matt Thorn, trans.

Wandering Son, volume 1

Fantagraphics, 2003. 202 p. ISBN: 9781606994160

VOLUME 1 IN THE WANDERING SON series introduces Nitori Shuichi and Takatsuki Yoshino. Both young fifth graders have a secret: the androgynous Shu wants to be a girl, and tomboy Yoshino wants to be a boy. The story follows them through their fifth-grade year as they mount a play in which the characters switch genders, the boys playing girls and the girls playing boys. Gradually Shu and Yoshino begin

experimenting with cross-dressing and feeling more comfortable in their new roles, though the ending of the novel is inconclusive, setting the stage for later volumes (seven at last count). The art is spare and attractive though the characters are sometimes difficult to tell apart. Shimura Takako is well known in Japan for her treatment of lesbian and transgender issues. Her exploration of the latter here is sweet spirited and insightful and provides arguably the only book for middle school–age readers to explore transgender identity. A useful guide to Japanese honorifics introduces the volume. **HV, GA**

Tamaki, Mariko and Jillian Tamaki
Skim
Groundwood Books, 2008. 141 p. ISBN: 9780888999641

IN THIS VERY DARK COMING-OF-AGE novel from Canada, Kim (whom everyone calls "Skim") is a mixed-race sixteen-year-old who goes to a girls' school along with her best friend, Lisa. Kim's interests are Wicca (she says she is "technically only starting to be a witch"), tarot cards (her card is the lovers reversed), astrology, and philosophy. But her real interest is her English/drama teacher, Ms. Archer, with whom she has fallen in love. But then the teacher unexpectedly departs for another school, leaving Kim bereft. At the same time a local boy, who is gay, commits suicide and Lisa decides Kim herself is suicidal. She's (probably) not, but she is definitely depressed, and her slice-of-life story is also a bit on the grim side, though there are hints of sunnier times ahead in the inconclusive ending. The story succeeds as a mood piece that focuses on the sometimes fraught emotional lives of a group of teenage girls, but the real success here is the fluid, black-and-white art, which perfectly captures the mood and tone of the text. The author and artist are cousins, and they obviously share the same sensibility. Much honored, *Skim* was selected by the *New York Times* as a Best Illustrated Children's Book and was also a YALSA Top Ten Great Graphic Novel for Teens. **HV**

Telgemeier, Raina

Drama

Graphix (Scholastic), 2012. 233 p. ISBN: 9780545326988

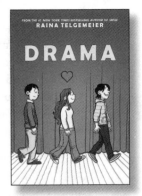

CALLIE LOVES THE THEATER and is thrilled to be backstage serving as set designer for her middle school's production of a musical titled *Moon over Mississippi*. Things are not going so well offstage, however. A (very) brief romance with Greg has soured, leaving Callie momentarily devastated, but then she meets identical twin brothers, Jesse and Justin. Ebullient, outgoing Jesse is openly gay, but his brother, quiet and shy Justin, is straight, and before she knows it, Callie has developed a serious crush on him. Jesse tries out for the musical and gets a major part, but Justin, who is an equally gifted actor, has stage fright and agrees to work backstage with Callie. When something disastrous happens the night of the play, Justin—to everyone's amazement—steps into the breach and plays the female lead's part to a thunderous ovation. When he then invites Callie to the school dance, she's elated until something else unexpected happens and it appears that perhaps Justin isn't straight after all. Happily, Callie accepts this, and she and Justin remain friends. Best of all, she is named stage manager for the next year's production, and the curtain closes on a happy ending. This is an absolutely delightful book in every way. It is funny, heartfelt, and captivating. Telgemeier has a wonderful gift for creating characters and, in her simple, full-color cartoon-like art, infusing them with personality. The book is also notable as being one of the few middle school titles to have gay content—and gay content handled with such charm and grace. **HV**

Vaughan, Brian K.

Runaways: Pride & Joy

2nd ed. Marvel, 2011. Unpaged. ISBN: 9780785157328

THIS FIRST OF THREE VOLUMES contains the first six issues of the Marvel series, which introduces six young people whose parents, unbeknownst to them, are super villains known, collectively, as The Pride. The kids discover the truth when they spy on their parents who have gathered, as they do annually, for a charity event. Soon they also discover that they have inherited their parents' superpowers and set out to defeat them. One of the teens, Karolina Dean, discovers she is an alien as readers discover she is also a lesbian. In later adventures she will begin a relationship with a new character, the shape-shifter Xavin. Creator Vaughan left the series after issue #24 and was replaced by Joss Whedon and, later, others. Clever and ingenious with attractive and engaging characters, *Runaways* is excellent entertainment. The only problem with this edition is its digest size, which reduces the type to such a small size as to be almost illegible. Volume 2 is titled *Teenage Wasteland*, and volume 3 is *Runaways Missing: The Good Die Young*. Other gay Marvel characters include partners Rictor and Shatterstar (see the various X-Factor books) and Hulkling and Wiccan (Young Avengers). **GA**

Williams III, J. H. and W. Haden Blackman

Batwoman Volume 1: Hydrology

DC Comics, 2013. Unpaged. ISBN: 9781401234652

CHILDREN OF GOTHAM CITY are being kidnapped, and it appears that the kidnapper is the legendary La Llo-rona, the Weeping Woman. Who can possibly stop her? Funny you should ask. Batwoman—aka Kate Kane—is on the case, helped by her lover, the beautiful police detective Sawyer, and her cousin Bette, aka Flamebird. But then, to further complicate an already complicated case, the Department of Extranormal Operations shows up with an offer that Batwoman may not be able to refuse, even if it puts her at odds with her cousin. Fans of superhero comics will embrace DC's latest effort, and gay readers will applaud the frank and open treatment of Batwoman's sexual iden-tity. The art is flamboyant, surging across double-page spreads like a wave. Though beautifully realized, it is sometimes overly hectic, making it difficult to "read." As for the text, readers unfamiliar with the characters and their backstories may feel like Batwoman herself, who at one point muses, "Feel like I'm walking into a movie in the middle . . . trying to catch up." All this aside, the introduction of an openly gay character into the DC universe is certainly cause for rejoicing and hoping that others will follow. **GA**

Winick, Judd

Pedro and Me: Friendship, Loss, and What I Learned

Holt, 2000. 187 p. ISBN: 9780805089646

CARTOONIST WINICK WAS A MEMBER of the cast of MTV's "The Real World: San Francisco." His roommate on the program was the HIV-positive AIDS educator Pedro Zamora. This affecting memoir of their friendship is a tribute to Zamora, who

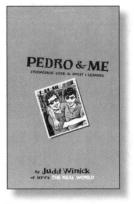

died at the age of twenty-two. Winick's narrative reflects the ways in which the MTV program became a de facto forum for educating the American public about being gay and living with AIDS. The story and its aftermath also tell of Winick's evolution as a cartoonist, his falling in love with another cast member, Pam Ling, and his own lecturing about AIDS. Winick is an excellent draftsman, and his black-and-white line drawings harmonize beautifully with the text, capturing and reflecting the often humorous, always compassionate mood and tone of this memorable book. **GA, QC**

Nonfiction

 **number of criteria are** used in evaluating informational (nonfiction) books for young readers. Nonfiction books should be visually inviting. The layout of text, images, graphics, sidebars, and other visual elements should engage the eye and work together for maximum clarity and reader engagement. The text should be accessible, the writing free of jargon. The language can be simple but never simplistic. The information must be factually accurate and as up-to-date as possible. Of course accuracy is a moving target over time, so recency may trump other concerns. For example, in 2003 a nonfiction book meets every criteria for nonfiction excellence and is added to a library's collection; in 2013 the same book may be discarded or replaced because, while it is still well written and visually engaging, the information it contains is ten years old. For some areas of nonfiction, such as books on legal or medical issues, a book that is even five years old is suspect. For other areas, such as biography or history, this may be less of a concern. For example, Russell Freedman's *Lincoln: A Photobiography* (Clarion, 1987) was published twenty-five-plus years ago and is still a valuable resource for young people seeking information about Abraham Lincoln. On the other hand, when the first edition of Margaret O. Hyde's *Know About AIDS* (Walker, 1987) appeared, it received high marks from reviewers as being "informative and useful" and having a "forthright style" and a

"clear, steady tone." The revised edition (Walker, 1990) was likewise praised, as was the third and final "completely revised" edition (Walker, 1994). Today, these books would no doubt be of interest to a historian studying the onset of the AIDS epidemic or the early years of AIDS education, but a twenty-five-plus-year-old book on AIDS would no longer be considered a source of current or reliable information.

The repeal of "Don't Ask, Don't Tell" in September 2011 created an immediate need for new or revised editions of books on gays in the military. More recently, informational books on same-sex marriage became no longer current when the US Supreme Court struck down the Defense of Marriage Act on June 2013. This does *not* mean these books should be discarded but simply that teen information seekers will need to consult (and librarians and educators will need to provide) more recent resources for current information on same-sex marriage. Future legislation, court cases, and judicial rulings will no doubt render other nonfiction YA titles with LGBTQ content obsolete, and (hopefully) spur the need for publishers to update online resources and publish new and revised editions of no-longer-current non-fiction. And that's *good*.

Over the past several decades, much has been written and said about "the death of the book" in a digital age. Governing boards, administrators, and consultants may declare that online information resources have rendered traditional books obsolete, but there are in fact some clear advantages to the traditional book format. This may be especially true for books with LGBTQ content, as this format is often better suited for teens' privacy concerns than other formats. If teens do not have access to a home computer, they may be understandably reluctant to access sites with LGBTQ content in a public setting like a school or public library. That said, online resources are invaluable to teens who need to find the most current information on their topic. And they can always tell onlookers that they are doing research for a school assignment!

The first nonfiction book about LGBTQ issues written for a teen audience, *A Way of Love, A Way of Life: A Young Person's Introduction to What It Means to Be Gay*, by Frances Hanckel and John Cunningham (Lothrop, Lee & Shepard) was published in 1979, ten years after the first fiction book with LGBTQ content appeared. At that time there were very few informational resources available to teens that did not present LGBTQ people as criminals, social deviants, or (at best) sad-eyed loners who needed to put more effort into becoming heterosexual.

There are now many informational resources that provide a range of LGBTQ-relevant information available in various print and electronic formats. The thirty-four books we highlight are all available in traditional print-on-paper editions, though some are also available as e-books. They include traditional nonfiction genres (biographies and memoirs, history, poetry, etc.) as well as information resources for LGBTQ teens and their allies on a personal level, a community level, and a national or international level.

The majority of the books listed in the following pages are considered young adult books; a smaller number were originally published for a middle grade or an adult audience. All are accessible to teen readers and will, we believe, stand the test of time. Well, for a while, anyway.

Books

Alsenas, Linas
Gay America: Struggle for Equality
Abrams/Amulet, 2008. 160 p. ISBN: 9780810994874

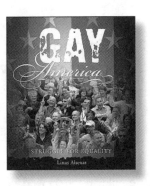

ALSENAS'S LANDMARK HISTORY OF AMERICAN gay life and culture focuses largely on public attitudes toward homosexuality and on the continuing struggle for gay rights. After a brief survey of social conditions in pre-twentieth-century America, the author narrows his focus to offer a closer examination of more recent events (through 2007). In an effort to humanize his material, Alsenas begins each chapter with an individual story told from a "personalized" (i.e., lightly fictionalized) point of view. While this succeeds in dramatizing factual material, the epic story the author tells of the gradual emergence of gays and lesbians from the shadows of public opprobrium is itself a compelling human drama. Alsenas's lively, engaging style makes his history very reader friendly, as do the many archival photographs that enliven each page. The first-ever book to cover this material for young adults, *Gay America* is essential reading for *all* young people.

Apelqvist, Eva
LGBTQ Families:
The Ultimate Teen Guide
Scarecrow Press, 2013. 197 p. ISBN: 9780810885363

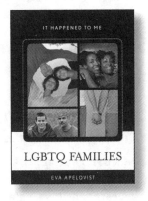

A VOLUME IN THE PUBLISHER'S It Happened to Me series, this useful and comprehensive volume is about what it's like to have LGBTQ parents. The author's research is supplemented by the many interviews she conducted with LGBTQ people and with their children and grandchildren. As the author acknowledges, "Injustice is a red thread throughout the pages, as it must be at this time in history,"

but her focus is much wider than this as she discusses such issues as sex and gender, love and marriage, legal issues, bullying, and much more. The book includes numerous sidebars ("From the Closet to the Courtroom," "Famous Out Olympians," "Overcoming Invisibility," etc.), photographic illustrations, profiles of LGBTQ families, and extensive notes. A glossary and a comprehensive list of resources are appended.

Aretha, David

No Compromise:
The Story of Harvey Milk

Morgan Reynolds Pub, 2009. 128 p.
ISBN: 9781599351292

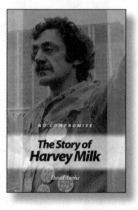

CALIFORNIA'S 1978 ELECTION BALLOTS INCLUDED Prop 6, a voter referendum that, if passed, would have made it illegal for any of the state's school districts to employ teachers who were gay or lesbian. The ultimate failure of Prop 6 was due in large part to Harvey Milk's savvy strategizing as a key member of the "No on 6" organization. Milk's public career was brief—he was assassinated after a year in office—but his work had a strong positive impact on the next generation of gay rights activists. The book's eight chapters tell the story of Harvey Milk's life and work, using numerous quotes from him and from others who knew him. The text is lively, engaging, and well documented, and the numerous photos enliven Milk's story still further. A time line, detailed source notes, a fifty-plus-item bibliography, and an index are also included. As one of the first openly gay people to be elected to political office, Harvey Milk was a pioneering gay rights activist who spoke eloquently on behalf of LGBTQ youth, his signature words being "You got to give them hope." Since Milk died more than two decades before current teens were born, his name may or may not be familiar to readers, but it should be.

Berlatsky, Noah

Homosexuality (Global Viewpoints)

Greenhaven Press, 2011. 224 p. ISBN: 9780737751925

AS NOTED ABOVE, THERE ARE few YA books with LGBTQ content having a non-US setting or focus. In fact, this volume in Greenhaven's Global Viewpoints series appears to be the single nonfiction YA book that offers an international perspective—in this case, through a collection of twenty-five previously published articles.

It would be impossible to represent more than a comparative handful of international perspectives in a volume of this sort, but the book's four sections contain articles on four broad subject areas: religious (eight pieces), cultural (five pieces), legal (seven pieces), and familial (five pieces). Nearly all are written by journalists and originally published in the twenty-first century; taken together they represent diverse perspectives from six continents. Additional resources are included in each section's bibliography, a total of forty articles from print and online sources, contact information for ten organizations with English-language websites, a bibliography of twenty-five adult books, discussion questions, and maps. It is unlikely that teens will consider this recreational reading, but the United States is still a nation of immigrants, and this accessible book will be invaluable as an information source on LGBTQ issues and events taking place in locations beyond the US border.

Bronski, Michael, Ann Pellegrini, and Michael Amico

"You Can Tell Just By Looking" and 20 Other Myths about LGBT Life and People

Beacon Press, 2013. 190 p. ISBN: 9780807042458

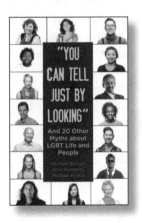

ONE OF THE BANES OF early YA LGBTQ books was the perpetuation of stereotypes and myths about gay and lesbian people: "It's just a phase," "Being gay will result in punishment (often by dying in a car crash)," "Lesbian and gay people are doomed to lives of loneliness lived on the farthest fringes of society," and so on. While some of these stereotypes and myths have been put to rest, others continue to flourish. Academics Bronski, Pellegrini, and Amico examine twenty of these in detail: "Can You Tell Who's Gay Just by Looking?" "LGBT Parents Are Bad for Children." "Transgender People Are Gay," and so on. As they state in their introduction, "This book is an attempt to help readers clear through the thicket of these and other hot-button issues. We want to dispel harmful, often hostile myths, stereotypes and false assumption about LGBT people." Sometimes, the authors stress, some of those assumptions are held by LGBTQ people themselves ("Homosexuals Are Born That Way"). In dispelling such myths, this book is an essential addition to LGBTQ literature and one that should be read by both straight and gay readers.

Chilman-Blair, Kim and John Taddeo

Medikidz Explain HIV

Rosen, 2010. 40 p. ISBN: 9781435894587

THE MEDIKIDZ ARE A MULTICULTURAL band of medical superheroes who educate readers via action-adventure and humor. The story begins at a soccer match: the score is tied and Matt is the player who, beset with HIV-related fatigue, misses a penalty kick. But wait—the Medikidz band spots Matt's distress and beams him up to their headquarters for a quick voyage through the bloodstream where he witnesses a battle between the immune system and an army of invading microbes. The superheroes are powerful, the dialog laced with humor, and Matt learns the importance of staying on top of his drug regimen. This may sound hopelessly didactic, but the Medikidz creators Chilman-Blair (doctor and medical educator) and Taddeo (former Marvel artist) have put together a winning team of superheroes and a winning story that uses action-adventure to provide clear information on retroviruses and how AZT and other drugs work to strengthen a weakened immune system. By the time Matt is beamed back to the soccer match, he has the knowledge he needs to stay healthy and prevent HIV from turning into full-blown AIDS. And this reader, at least, has a clear and understandable model representing the complex cellular-level dance of retroviruses, T-cells, microbes, and antibodies that comprise the immune system. The book includes sidebars and a glossary plus a list of websites and other resources on HIV/AIDS. Highly recommended for ages ten and up.

Eaklor, Vicki L.

Queer America: A People's GLBT History of the United States

Greenwood, 2008. 274 p. ISBN: 9781595586360

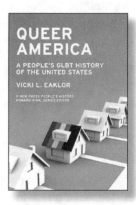

THIS IS A CHRONOLOGICAL ACCOUNT of twentieth-century LGBTQ history within the larger context of US and world history. The opening chapter provides a rationale for teaching this history. This may be of limited interest to teens, but teachers will find it useful in making a persuasive case for the study of LGBTQ history. The eight chapters that follow provide relevant and engagingly presented information in a decade-by-decade account of twentieth-century history. At the end of each chapter is a one-to-two-page boxed text that presents specific questions and arguments that arise in considering that particular time period. For example, the chapter on the 1960s ends with the question, "How important was the Stonewall Riot?" Other questions are raised and debated in other time periods. During World Wars I and II: "Should homosexuals serve in the military?" During the 1980s: "Should public figures be outed?" During the 1990s: "Is there a gay gene?" One or more contemporaneous photos add visual interest to each chapter. This comprehensive text is a useful companion to Alsenas's text (above), which is geared toward younger readers.

Franco, Betsy, ed.

Falling Hard:
100 Love Poems by Teenagers

Candlewick Press, 2008. 160 p. ISBN: 9780763634377

COLLECTED BY E-MAIL FROM THE United States and abroad, these 100 poems are written by a catholic collection of contributors: straight and gay, bisexual and transgender teens, ranging in age from twelve to eighteen. Their work—celebratory, emotional, evocative, happy, and sad—evokes the many aspects and meanings of love. Mostly written in free verse, though also in rap and rhyme, the poems range in length from one line ("I am the flour to your tortilla, baby.") to several pages. Though the poems range in quality, they are one in their eloquence and emotional honesty. An excellent collection for readers both in and out of love.

Gay, Kathlyn

Bigotry and Intolerance:
The Ultimate Teen Guide

It Happened to Me series #35. Scarecrow, 2013. 175 p.
ISBN: 9780810883604

THIS AMBITIOUS—AND LARGELY SUCCESSFUL—book takes on a number of loaded terms and provides specific information about bigotry, intolerance, prejudice, stereotypes, "hate speech," and other words used in discussions of discrimination on the basis of insider/outsider status within and between groups. The first chapter, "What's a bigot?" provides a working definition: "someone who is strongly partial to his or her own group, religion, race, or politics and intolerant of those who differ." The book's ten chapters explore historical and contemporary issues of intolerance based on perceived differences (e.g., religion, race, sexuality, national origin, ability/disability). One of the book's strengths is its reader-friendly format: each chapter includes several boxed texts with examples that illustrate the impact of bigotry on individuals and groups, including individuals' stories (e.g., a boy who comes out to his parents and is sent to an antigay bootcamp to "turn him straight"); historical events (e.g.,: the internment of Japanese-Americans during World War II); "What do you think?" descriptions of recent First Amendment controversies; and descriptive annotations of recommended books and movies on these and other subjects. An up-to-date list of thoughtfully chosen articles, books, websites, and organizations is included.

Greenberg, Jan and Sandra Jordan
Andy Warhol: Prince of Pop
Delacorte Press, 2004. 208 p. ISBN: 9780385730563

"IN THE FUTURE EVERYBODY WILL be world famous for fifteen minutes."—Andy Warhol (1928–1987). This biography of Warhol, visual and conceptual artist, filmmaker, director, and public figure, provides the reader with a clear and well-documented narrative of his life and work. Although he died nearly thirty years ago, his iconic depictions of popular culture (multiple images of soup cans and dollar bills; portraits of Marilyn Monroe, Jacqueline Kennedy Onassis, and other media stars) are immediately recognizable by viewers whose knowledge of contemporary art ranges from extensive to nonexistent. The authors' research and writing skill are evident throughout in an absorbing and accessible narrative of Warhol's life and work that includes his impoverished and sickly childhood in working class Pittsburgh; early evidence of his artistic talent; his restless—and often opportunistic—determination to succeed as both artist and celebrity, and, yes, his lifelong attraction to other men. The book's twenty chapters are supplemented by a thirty-two-page section of black-and-white photos and color reproductions of Warhol's life and work, a timeline, glossary of artists and art terms, extensive source notes, bibliography, mediography, and index.

Hartzler, Aaron

Rapture Practice: My One-Way Ticket to Salvation. A True Story

Little, Brown, 2013. 400 p. ISBN: 9780316094658

HARTZLER'S ENGAGING MEMOIR CHARTS the course of his coming-of-age in a conservative Christian family that expects the Rapture (i.e., the bodily ascent into heaven before Armageddon) to arrive at any moment. It's a given that there will be no secular pleasures—movies, music, TV—in his young life. At first the proverbial best little boy in the world, he gradually becomes quietly rebellious, secretly listening to secular music, going to movies, drinking, and gradually coming to question his family's beliefs. And oh yes: experiencing a growing awareness that he might be attracted to boys. Despite what most readers will view as the oppressive nature of his home life, Hartzler's memoir is rooted in love and enlivened by welcome humor. An open ending invites the possibility of a sequel in which he might further examine his sexuality.

Hernandez, Daniel with Susan Goldman Rubin

They Call Me a Hero: A Memoir of My Youth

Simon & Schuster, 2013. 240 p. ISBN: 9781442462281

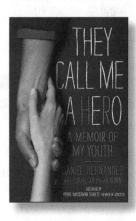

A COMING-OF-AGE MEMOIR, *THEY CALL Me a Hero* limns the early life of the twenty-year-old political intern to US Representative Gabby Giffords. When she was shot on January 8, 2011, he was the first to reach her, administered first aid (likely saving her life), rode with her in the ambulance, and called her friends to report the shooting. Written by Rubin, the book is based on extensive interviews with Hernandez, a gay Latino, who shares details of the attempted assassination and the next six months of ceremonies, interviews, speeches, and meetings with President Obama. Hernandez recalls his growing up in Tucson, mastering English, and being bullied because of his size, sexuality, and Mexican-American background. Hernandez is laudably modest about his role in saving Giffords: "I felt shy about accepting the title of 'hero,' but I was beginning to learn how to take the compliments." His courage and continuing commitment to public service are inspiring.

Huegel, Kelly

GLBTQ: The Survival Guide for Queer & Questioning Teens

Free Spirit, 2003. 240 p. ISBN: 9781575421261

HUEGEL'S IS AN INDISPENSABLE GUIDE for gay, lesbian, bisexual, transgender, and questioning teens, as well as for their straight peers and their parents and other adult caregivers. In her eleven candid, fact-filled, nonjudgmental chapters, she covers every aspect of LGBTQ—from coming out to homophobia, from religion and culture to sex and sensibility. Happily, she devotes an entire chapter to being transgender, a condition of being that is too often ignored in books for teens. The tone throughout is supportive and matter-of-fact. Hegel's recommendations are sensible and practical, while apposite quotations from young people who have "been there" enrich the text. Designed for browsing, the book also contains an extraordinary number of references to additional resources—many of them online—as well as a glossary and a bibliography. This is one of the best one-volume sources of information about being LGBTQ and is highly recommended.

Hyde, Sue

Come Out and Win: Organizing Yourself, Your Community, and Your World

Beacon Press, 2007. 168 p. ISBN: 9780807079720

IN THE WORDS OF FORMER US Congressman Barney Frank, "Winning equal rights for LGBT people is not a spectator sport." But where to start? How to begin? Sue Hyde, longtime political activist with the National Gay and Lesbian Task Force, offers information, advice, and strategies based on several decades of activism within and on behalf of LGBTQ communities. Each information-rich chapter focuses on a key element of organizing and community building, starting with "Chapter 1: I/You/We: The Three Pronouns of Coming Out," which begins with an individual's decision to come out, a personal process that may lay the groundwork for activism on behalf of those engaged in similar struggles. The author uses a Big Picture question, What will it take to erase homophobia? to introduce a step-by-step process for organizing for change, plus a "game plan" for specific projects, including "Try this at home: Organize a gay-straight alliance at your school." The six chapters that follow cover other essential elements of working effectively with individuals and in groups (e.g., communicating your message, building coalitions). Each chapter includes further advice, resources, and a practical game plan for getting the job(s) done.

James, Otto

AIDS (Voices series)

Smart Apple Media, 2009. 46 p. ISBN: 9781599202822

THIS ACCESSIBLE BOOK PROVIDES A useful overview of HIV/AIDS and the global impact of the AIDS epidemic. The text is organized around a series of eighteen succinct questions, each addressed by a visually engaging two-page spread that includes text, color photos, graphs, charts, boxed information, and quotes from organizations (e.g., the World Health Organization, the US Centers for Disease Control and Prevention), individuals involved in HIV/AIDS education and treatment (e.g., health care workers, educators) and individuals whose lives have been directly affected by HIV/AIDS (e.g., people living with AIDS and their families, people in high-risk populations). Although each section includes text and images from up to ten different sources, the graphic design makes each surprisingly easy to navigate via skillful use of fonts, text sizes, and visual arrangement. The photos and quotes are from more than twenty different countries on nearly every continent. Two of the eighteen questions address the specific concerns of LGBTQ communities: "Is AIDS a gay disease?" and "Is AIDS God's judgment?" These two questions receive the same amount of attention as the other sixteen questions. This helpful text can be used to replace myths and misinformation with solid facts about the ongoing fight against AIDS on an international level.

Kenan, Randall and Amy Sickels

James Baldwin (Gay and Lesbian Writers series)

Chelsea House, 2005. 150 p. ISBN: 9780791082218

THIS BOOK'S 150 PAGES PROVIDE a brief but informative look at the life and work of James Baldwin (1924–1987), novelist, essayist, and black gay man. The book opens with a description of Baldwin's 1963 trip to Selma, Alabama, to aid in the black voter registration drive. As a best-selling author and powerful speaker on behalf of racial

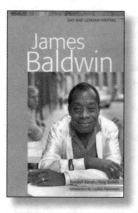

justice, Baldwin was invited to Selma to bring increased media attention to the difficulties black Americans faced in simply registering to vote. At the same time, Baldwin's presence was a direct challenge to the power of Selma's White Citizens Council. The physical danger he faced in Selma was genuine, as was Baldwin's courage. The text is based on published sources and includes frequent quotes from Baldwin's works as well as those of his other biographers. Previous studies of Baldwin written for young people have made little-to-no mention of his sexual identity, so this book acts as a corrective, and libraries that include other biographies of Baldwin may want to acquire this one as well. An earlier edition of this text (Chelsea House, 1993) was enhanced by numerous photos and other visual material. Unfortunately, the 2005 edition contains no images, which may limit the book's appeal to some teens, but it includes boxed texts (on the Freedom Riders, the Black Panthers, Greenwich Village's gay and lesbian scene, and others) with additional information about Baldwin's life and times. As Baldwin stated in a 1970 interview, "I'm a witness. That's my responsibility. I write it all down."

Kuhn, Betsy

Gay Power!: The Stonewall Riots and the Gay Rights Movement, 1969

21st Century Books, 2011. 144 p. ISBN: 9780761357681

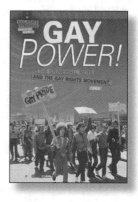

A VOLUME IN THE PUBLISHER'S Civil Rights Struggles around the World series, *Gay Power!* examines LGBTQ people's struggle for civil rights from colonial America to the present. The author gives particular attention to what has become known as The Stonewall Riots. In 1969 New York City police raided a gay bar called the Stonewall Inn, and to their surprise, the normally quiescent gay customers fought back, throwing rocks and bottles and chanting "Gay Power." The result was the beginning of the gay liberation movement, which endures to the present day. In addition to Stonewall, she addresses such considerations as religion (the founding of the Metropolitan Community Church); the removal by the American Psychiatric Association of homosexuality from its list of mental illnesses; AIDS; gay marriage; and more. This valuable contribution to LGBTQ history is enhanced by its inclusion of a comprehensive timeline, a glossary, a who's who of gay rights leaders, source notes, a selected bibliography and recommendations for further reading, films, and websites.

Kuklin, Susan

Beyond Magenta:
Transgender Teens Speak Out

Candlewick Press, 2014. 182 p. ISBN: 9780763656119

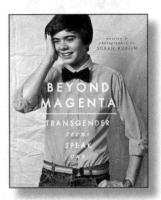

"'WHAT ARE YOU? . . . PINK OR BLUE?' / and I said I'm a real nice color of magenta." These words are drawn from a poem by Luke, one of the six transgender teens featured in Kuklin's groundbreaking book. Each of the six chapters tells the story of one of these teens via first person narratives based on transcribed interviews plus unobtrusive backstory details added by Kuklin. At birth, four of the teens were designated male, two female, but all share a lifelong sense of nonconformity/alienation from traditional binary sex/gender designations; otherwise they are diverse in terms of race, class, culture, and family configuration. The conversational interviews provide memorable details of each teen's life: past, present, and anticipated future. Five stories are enhanced by Kuklin's sensitive photographic portraits (most in color), while the author's extensive story-behind-the-story notes provide additional context for her subjects' lives. This important and accessible book brings welcome clarity to a subject that has often been obscure and gives faces literally and metaphorically to a long-invisible segment of the teen population. Six individuals cannot represent all transgender teens, but it's a start. As Jessy says, "So forget the category. Just talk to me. Get to know me."

Levithan, David and Billy Merrell, eds.

The Full Spectrum: A New Generation of Writing about Gay, Lesbian, Bisexual, Transgender, Questioning, and Other Identities

Knopf, 2006. 288 p. ISBN: 0375832904

THE FORTY CONTRIBUTIONS TO THIS invaluable collection about personal identity have two things in common: all are nonfiction and all are by writers under the age of twenty-three. Beyond that, diversity is the order of the day, and the result is a vivid demonstration of how extraordinarily broad the full spectrum of sexual identity is among today's gay, lesbian, bisexual, transgender, and questioning youth.

Some of the material in these essays and poems will be familiar (the agony of coming out, the heartbreak of religious opprobrium), but what is new and encouraging is that so many young people have felt free to share the truth about themselves in print and under their own names. As coeditor Levithan notes in his introduction, "One way to effect change is to share truths. To tell our stories." Insightful, extraordinarily well written, and emotionally mature, the selections offer compelling, dramatic evidence that what is important in life is not what we are but who we are.

Marcus, Eric

What If? Answers to Questions about What It Means to Be Gay and Lesbian

Simon & Schuster, 2013. 192 p. ISBN: 9781442482982

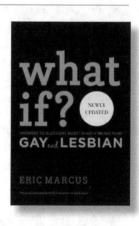

MARCUS'S INTELLIGENT GUIDE TO WHAT it means to be gay and lesbian remains an indispensable introduction to an occasionally thorny subject. Though much of the material here will be familiar to readers of the 2007 edition, there is enough new content to warrant purchase of this updated version with its slightly new title. As before, the material is divided topically (e.g., Friends and Family, Sex, School). And the thoughtful answers to many of his questions (e.g., "How do people react when they find out a friend is gay?" "My two moms had a commitment ceremony. Is that the same thing as getting married?") are enriched by the inclusion of anecdotal material derived from the author's own experience or from interviews with teens and caring adults. In addition to new material about transgender people, gay marriage, religion, and education, the chapter on resources has been substantially updated and expanded. Whether old or new, the content of Marcus's Q&A guide remains lucid, fair, and laudably commonsensical.

Mastoon, Adam

The Shared Heart: Portraits and Stories Celebrating Lesbian, Gay, and Bisexual Young People

HarperTeen, 2001. 192 p. ISBN: 9780064473040

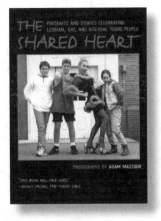

THIS BOOK WAS FIRST PUBLISHED in 1997 as an oversized hardcover with medium-weight paper suitable for crisp photographic reproduction of Mastoon's black-and-white portraits of the forty LGBTQ youth (ages sixteen to twenty-two) featured in this book. Most are pictured alone, three are with their parents, and one photo is a group shot of four standing in front of a college dormitory. Each portrait is accompanied by a first-person narrative of that person's coming out story plus a brief handwritten note from them. In 2001 the book was reissued as a mass market paperback. The content is exactly the same with one significant difference: the cover of the 1997 edition featured a photo of Don, a handsome young white teen. His handwritten words begin, "I think a great deal of stress is lifted when you come out . . ." The cover photo of the 2001 edition also features Don—he's one of the four teens in the group shot. This time his words begin, "Yo, I'm Don . . . ." A still current and invaluable book for all teens who want to view, read, and meet forty young, diverse LGBTQ people, all of whom have something important to say.

Miller, Calvin Craig

No Easy Answers: Bayard Rustin and the Civil Rights Movement

Morgan Reynolds, 2005. 160 p. ISBN: 9781931798433

THE APTLY TITLED NO EASY ANSWERS is a straightforward look at the life of Bayard Rustin (1912–1987), a remarkable but too-little known African-American activist whose work was critical to the success of the Civil Rights Movement. This book's 160 pages trace the career of Rustin from his early years through his lifelong career working on behalf of racial equality and nonviolence. He was an astute political strategist whose persuasive arguments were directly responsible for Dr. Martin Luther King Jr.'s decision to adopt nonviolence as a winning strategy during and after the Montgomery bus boycott. In 1953, however, he was arrested in California for "indecent acts" in a police sweep of gay clubs and neighborhoods. His arrest—a misdemeanor—was made public, and Rustin became "openly gay." The book's narrative starts in the days immediately before the 1963 March on Washington. Rustin is unflappable as he coordinates the innumerable logistical tasks required for the march to be considered a success, well aware that success would be judged not only by the thousands of march participants, but also by the millions of people who would be observing the march and speeches in the media. This was a day when the whole world really *was* watching. Rustin was a savvy activist who knew that his strength lay in the behind-the-scenes work of the Civil Rights Movement. Rustin also knew that—as a "known homosexual"—his presence in the movement was a potential liability. As a result, the story of Bayard Rustin is a little-known one, and it is most encouraging to see his story told—and well told—in a book for a teen audience.

Moon, Sarah, ed.

The Letter Q: Queer Writers' Notes to Their Younger Selves

Scholastic, 2012. 272 p. ISBN: 9780545399326

THE LETTER Q STANDS FOR "Queer," of course, and in this lovely, often funny, and always heartfelt book, more than five dozen celebrated authors write letters to their teenage selves. Each letter, in its own individual way, promises the author's younger self hope that, in the future, life will get better. In a moving introduction editor Sarah Moon offers her own personal testimony to that. The assembled authors, actors, playwrights, and illustrators are a veritable who's who of the LGBTQ creative world that include authors for both young adult and adult readers. In the former category are such talents as Julie Anne Peters, Jacqueline Woodson, David Levithan, and others. Not every author in the latter category will be familiar to teens but whether familiar or not, they are an amazing array of talent—Michael Cunningham, Terrence McNally, Paul Rudnick, David Leavitt, and more. Appended brief biographies of the contributors provide necessary introductions and background information. Readers who enjoy this will want to read Dan Savage and Terry Miller's *It Gets Better* (below).

Newman, Leslea

October Mourning:
A Song for Matthew Shepard

Candlewick Press, 2012. 128 p. ISBN: 9780763658076

ON OCTOBER 6, 1998, TWENTY-ONE-YEAR-OLD Matthew Shepard, a gay student at the University of Wyoming, was lured into a truck, driven into the country, savagely beaten, tied to a fence and left to die—which he did five days later. In this collection of sixty-eight powerful poems, Leslea Newman recreates the events and circumstances surrounding this unspeakably vile hate crime. In so doing so she has created a moving tribute to a young man she regards as a martyr. Her poems are told from multiple points of view—including, boldly, that of the fence, the rope that bound the boy, and a doe who stood watch over him. The beautifully realized poems are also written in a variety of different forms ranging from haiku to villanelle, from concrete poetry to rhymed couplets. Each form (they're discussed in an appendix) matches the tone and mood of its content, creating an almost musical effect that is intellectually and emotionally engaging. Written with love, anger, regret, and other deeply felt emotions, *October Mourning* is a truly important book that deserves the widest readership, not only among independent readers but among students in a classroom setting. Most important, however, the book will introduce Matthew Shepard to a generation of readers who are too young to remember the tragic circumstances of his death and, thus, keep his name alive.

Paprocki, Sherry Beck

Ellen DeGeneres: Entertainer
(Women of Achievement series)

Chelsea House Publishers, 2009. 136 p.
ISBN: 9781604130829

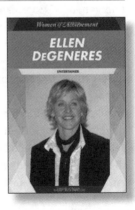

GIVEN HER POPULARITY WITH VIEWERS of all ages, a number of Ellen DeGeneres biographies written for a teen audience have appeared over the past several years. Most range from OK to pretty OK, but if a reader or a collection is limited to a single biography of DeGeneres, this is the one to have. Here is an engaging and information-rich biography of actress, comedian, and talk show host Ellen DeGeneres, whose sitcom character's widely publicized coming out episode in 1997 put her in the forefront of the struggle for LGBTQ visibility in network television. The outcome: six months later her show was cancelled, and it appeared Ellen's television career was over. Like other Chelsea House biographies, the book opens with an account of a significant event in the subject's life. The book certainly includes these events in 1997, but it opens ten years later as she hosts another episode of her highly successful daytime television talk show. The significant event here isn't the crisis of coming out but what her life became after the crisis was over, when her career again took a turn and her talk show was an immediate success. Each of the book's eight chapters includes two or three color photos; the text also includes a chronology, source notes, bibliography, resources, and an index.

Rachel, T. Cole and Rita D. Costello, eds.

Bend, Don't Shatter: Poets on the Beginning of Desire

Soft Skull Press/Red Rattle Books, 2004. 111 p.
ISBN: 9781932360172

THIS ANTHOLOGY OF WORK BY forty-three poets (fifteen female, twenty-eight male) was published in 2004 and has held up well over time as a vivid representation of the perceptions and experiences of queer youth. In a brief introduction, the editors note that young people commonly turn to poetry during adolescence, and this book provides ample incentive for doing so. No author bios are included, so few certain generalizations can be made about these poets, but their words give evidence of a diverse group of LGBTQ poets in terms of culture, class, religion, race, and location, who took a range of paths toward adulthood. The fifty-nine poems here are brief (nearly half are complete on one page) explorations of intense emotion, sharp observation, and slow or sudden realizations drawn from each writer's lived experience. The free verse texts (from hip-hop rhythms to more traditional cadences) span a range of emotions and perspectives, but clearly, this is not the "love that dare not speak its name" of earlier generations. Like Whitman, they celebrate themselves; not in the coded language of the past, but in straightforward descriptions of the insights and feelings of LGBTQ youth in the process of recognizing themselves (and their kindred spirits) as they turn toward the future.

Savage, Dan and Terry Miller, eds.

It Gets Better: Coming Out, Overcoming Bullying, and Creating a Life Worth Living

Plume, 2012. 338 p. ISBN: 9780525952336

IN RESPONSE TO A SPATE of LGBT teen suicides, columnist and author Savage and his partner Miller posted a video to YouTube in which they talked about how they survived bullying during their teen years to become successful adults. The video launched the It Gets Better Project on YouTube, which has inspired and generated more than 10,000 videos from gay and straight adults including numerous celebrities. Especially notable is one from President Obama. All of the videos are loving, caring, and compassionate and have been adapted and expanded into the essays that comprise this memorable and valuable book that deserves the widest possible readership.

Setterington, Ken

Branded by the Pink Triangle

Second Story Press, 2013. 141 p. ISBN: 9781926920962

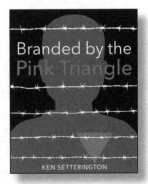

THOUGH HOMOSEXUALITY HAD BEEN ILLEGAL in Germany since 1871, Berlin was widely regarded as the gay capital of Europe in the early twentieth century and attitudes toward homosexuals were generally relaxed, even tolerant. All that changed with the rise of Nazism in the 1930s, when persecution of gays became the order of the day and, with the creation of concentration camps, many were remanded to this living death, forced to wear pink triangles on their clothing to identify them as being gay. No one knows how many gays died in the camps, but the mortality rate is estimated to be as high as sixty percent. Setterington, a librarian, has written an informative, well-researched, and documented history of the brutal treatment of homosexuals at the hands of the Nazis, humanizing his account with stories of survivors who have written about their experiences. His account also includes an overview of the distressing condition of being gay in postwar Germany and, finally, brings the story up to date with a hopeful chapter titled "It Gets Better." Setterington's is a significant contribution to LGBTQ history and one that deserves a wide readership.

Shepard, Judy with Jon Barrett

The Meaning of Matthew: My Son's Murder in Laramie, and a World Transformed

Hudson Street Press/Penguin, 2009. 273 p.
ISBN: 9781616847581

THE WORLD WAS SHOCKED WHEN the brutal murder of twenty-one-year-old college student Matthew Shepard (he was beaten for being gay and left for dead) was discovered. Ten years after the event his mother's courageous and moving narrative revisits the tragedy and explores its far-reaching impact. She prefaces the event with a discussion of Matthew's childhood, his being beaten and raped in Morocco on a high school trip, and his subsequent depression. She writes of the media circus that followed her son's death and of the subsequent capture and trial of his murderers. In its wake she has become a tireless advocate for LGBTQ causes, tolerance, and hate-crime legislation. Her powerful memoir is essential reading for both straight and LGBTQ teens.

Solomon, Steven

Homophobia: Deal with It and Turn Prejudice into Pride

Lorimer, 2013. 32 p. ISBN: 9781459404427

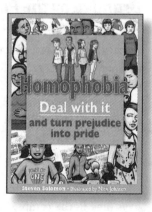

"WHETHER YOU ARE GAY OR straight, you can be affected by homophobia. And this book can help you identify and deal with people who are homophobic." This Canadian import's brevity and comic book format provide an unusual approach to the difficult topic of antigay prejudice, but it's a difficulty teens regularly encounter in the knee-jerk "that's so gay!" homophobic environment of many secondary schools. The author addresses readers directly with wry humor, offering useful information via examples, scenarios, Q&As, advice column letters, and true-false and multiple-choice quizzes.

The book starts with "Homophobia 101," a description of homophobia's various forms and impacts in the lives of teens. What follows is a closer look at homophobic incidents from three perspectives—the target, the homophobe, and the witness—and strategic advice to teens familiar with these dismal dynamics who could use a fresh perspective. Teens hear "it gets better," but what about right now? Here is information for understanding, coping with, and—who knows?—maybe even improving that right now. Antigay prejudice affects all of us; this would-be is a useful addition to public, middle school, and high school libraries.

Sonenklar, Carol

AIDS

Lerner, 2011. 128 p. ISBN: 9780822585817

THE SEVEN CHAPTERS OF THIS clearly written and abundantly illustrated resource provide an information-rich overview of the AIDS health crisis, including its history, symptoms, treatment, living with AIDS, AIDS as an international health crisis, current research and funding, and emerging issues. Threaded through the book, the ongoing stories of three individuals who are directly affected by HIV/AIDS raise readers' awareness of the lives behind the medical statistics: a pregnant woman discovers that she is HIV-positive; a newly out teen learns his current boyfriend is HIV-positive; and an adopted eleven-year-old girl finds out that her mother died of AIDS and that she herself is HIV-positive. The book's visually arresting format combines text with news photos, graphs, portraits, boxed sidebars, and relevant stories from *USA Today*. The book includes a glossary, a list of resources, websites, a bibliography, further reading, and an index. This title is part of the twelve-volume "*USA Today*'s Health Reports: Diseases and Disorders" series, each of which explores health issues currently in the news (and familiar to teens: anorexia and bulimia, anxiety disorders, asthma, OCD) in an accessible and teen-friendly format.

Vitagliano, Paul

Born This Way: Real Stories of Growing Up Gay

Quirk Books, 2012. 128 p. ISBN: 9781594745997

THIS COMPILATION OF NEARLY 100 entries comes from the author's Born This Way blog (bornthiswayblog.com). Each entry includes a brief personal story about growing up LGBTQ plus a childhood photo of the storyteller, the contributor's age and location, and the year the photo was taken. As a whole, the group is homogenous in some ways and diverse in others. All but two were born after 1950; most—but not all—are white; and three-quarters are male. Their class and cultural backgrounds vary, as do their urban/suburban/rural settings and geographic locations.

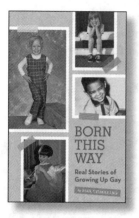

A full one-third of the contributors grew up in four states (California, New York, Ohio, and Texas), but the other two-thirds describe childhoods spent in twenty-four states and eight countries. Some of these color snapshots and school photos picture kids with attitude: visibly cross-gender (boys in drag voguing for the camera, girls in cowboy outfits) or in more traditional gendered attire. The emphasis here is on humor: children in costume as cha-cha dancers, trick-or-treaters, or Dracula; holding a just-caught fish or a pink Easter purse; wearing black galoshes and a smile; a carnation boutonniere and a scowl. These candid photos and accompanying stories reflect the expressive moments and subversive delight of children at play *before* they navigate their way through painful teenage self-consciousness to emerge as successful "born this way" adults. As Marco, who grew up in Italy in the 1960s, notes, "It is important to show who you really are without fear, because your photos will always show it anyway."

Wahls, Zach with Bruce Littlefield

My Two Moms: Lessons of Love, Strength, and What Makes a Family

Gotham Books, 2012. 256 p. ISBN: 9781592407132

"THE SEXUAL ORIENTATION OF MY parents has had zero effect on the content of my character." So testified then-nineteen-year-old Eagle Scout Zach Wahls before the Iowa House Judiciary Committee in 2011. His testimony went viral and quickly became YouTube's number one political video for 2011. His subsequent memoir examines the experience of growing up in a nontraditional family headed by two loving female parents. Wahls devotes each chapter to a value named in the Boy Scout Law (e.g., obedience, kindness, reverence, helpfulness, loyalty, thriftiness, and bravery) and focuses on the role that each value has played in his life as he traces his traditional childhood in Iowa and his years as a Boy Scout. Wahls offers an evenhanded and stirring defense of his nontraditional family. No stranger to bullying himself, he became a secondary school student leader, participating in sports, captaining his school's speech and debate team, and yes, attaining the rank of Eagle Scout. This is essential reading for anyone interested in LGBTQ families.

Youth Communication

Out with It: Gay and Straight Teens Write About Homosexuality

Youth Communication, 2009. 156 p.

ISBN: 9781933939728

ACCEPTANCE AND LOVE ARE THE recurring themes of this compilation of a dozen personal stories from both LGBTQ and straight teen contributors. Powerful and resonant ("My love is as valid as any straight person's"), the selections are unsparing in their candid depictions of coming out, homophobia, and sexuality. Youth Communication is a New York–based nonprofit youth media organization that seeks to help marginalized youth develop their full potential through reading and writing.

Professional Resources

D **uring the past decade,** a number of books have been published that focus on LGBTQ teens from the perspective of teachers, librarians, counselors, parents, and other adults who work with them or are interested in learning how to best serve their needs. With this in mind, we have chosen recently published books that contain information on recommended resources, services, and educational settings endorsed by professionals currently working with LGBTQ youth. As professional resources, they are addressed to adults, though LGBTQ teens may find them useful and immediately relevant to their personal needs.

Biegel, Stuart. *The Right to Be Out: Sexual Orientation and Gender Identity in America's Public Schools.* University of Minnesota Press, 2010. 300 p. ISBN: 9780816674589.

Cart, Michael and Christine A. Jenkins. *The Heart Has Its Reasons: Young Adult Literature with Gay/Lesbian/Queer Content, 1969–2004.* Scarecrow Press: Scarecrow Studies in Young Adult Literature series, 2006. 232 p. ISBN: 9780810850712.

Cianciotto, Jason and Sean Cahill. *LGBT Youth in America's Schools*. University of Michigan Press, 2012. 248 p. ISBN: 9780472031405.

DeWitt, Peter. *Dignity for All: Safeguarding LGBT Students*. Corwin Press, 2012. 117 p. ISBN: 9781452205908.

Greenblatt, Ellen, ed. *Serving LGBTIQ Library and Archives Users: Essays on Outreach, Service, Collections and Access*. McFarland, 2011. 346 p. ISBN: 9780786448944.

Kidd, Kenneth and Michelle Ann Abate, eds. *Over the Rainbow: Queer Children's and Young Adult Literature*. University of Michigan Press, 2011. 407 p. ISBN: 9780472051465.

Marcus, Eric. *Is It a Choice? Answers to the Most Frequently Asked Questions about Gay and Lesbian People*. HarperSanFrancisco, 2005. 258 p. ISBN: 9780060832803.

Martin, Hillias J. and James R. Murdock. *Serving Lesbian, Gay, Bisexual, Transgender, and Questioning Teens: A How-To-Do-It Manual for Librarians #151*. Neal-Schuman Publishers, 2007. 267 p. ISBN: 9781555705664.

Mayo, Cris. *LGBTQ Youth and Education: Policies and Practices*. Teachers College Press, Columbia University, 2014. 145 p. ISBN: 9780807754887.

Naidoo, Jamie Campbell. *Rainbow Family Collections: Selecting and Using Children's Books with Lesbian, Gay, Bisexual, Transgender, and Queer Content*. ABC-CLIO and Libraries Unlimited, 2012. 260 p. ISBN: 9781598849608.

Serwatka, Thomas S. *Queer Questions, Clear Answers: The Contemporary Debates on Sexual Orientation*. Praeger/ABC-CLIO, 2010. 265 p. ISBN: 9780313386121.

Vaccaro, Annemarie, Gerri August, and Megan S. Kennedy. *Safe Spaces: Making Schools and Communities Welcoming to LGBT Youth*. Prager, 2011. 192 p. ISBN: 9780313393686.

Webber, Carlisle K. *Gay, Lesbian, Bisexual, Transgender and Questioning Teen Literature: A Guide to Reading Interests*. Libraries Unlimited: Genreflecting Advisory Series, 2010. 131 p. ISBN: 9781591585060.

Fiction Codes: Tracking Trends over Time

E ACH FICTION TITLE IN THIS BOOK HAS ONE OR MORE CODES (HV, GA, and QC) that place it in the larger continuum of young adult literature with LGBTQ content. HV stands for "homosexual visibility," GA for "gay assimilation," and QC for "queer consciousness/community." Readers may wonder about the origin and meaning of these categories.

Both of us have been seeking out, reading, and evaluating young adult books with LGBTQ content since the late 1970s. At the outset, neither of us found more than a handful of such books, and most of that handful were predictably grim "problem novels" in which LGBTQ issues were the symptoms or the cause of the teen protagonist's troubles. Before we met in person (Jenkins lived in Michigan, Cart in California), we read each other's articles on the topic and began a correspondence, evaluating current titles and sharing our new discoveries.

In 2000 we decided to collaborate on creating a comprehensive picture of this literature from its earliest years to the present. The result was *The Heart Has Its Reasons: Young Adult Literature with Gay/Lesbian/Queer Content, 1969–2004*.[1] In addition to describing individual books, we wanted to bring to light overall patterns in this literature over time. What sort of stories included LGBTQ characters? How were they portrayed? How have their portrayals and the story lines changed (or not) as society has become more accepting of LGBTQ people?

In seeking a model to understand this literature over time, Jenkins turned to Rudine Sims Bishop's remarkable *Shadow and Substance: Afro-American Experience in Contemporary Children's Fiction*,[2] a groundbreaking analysis of children's books with African-American characters published from 1964 to 1984. Sims Bishop proposed a three-part model to describe changing representations of African-American characters in children's books during the two decades immediately following the enactment of the Civil Rights Act of 1964. The first books to appear were what she termed *social conscience* books, in which a single African-American child or family moves to a previously all-white school or neighborhood. In these stories of racial integration, prejudice is the problem, and desegregation the solution. Once the process of racial integration begins, previously hostile—or simply clueless—characters learn that they had in fact prejudged each other based on faulty assumptions of insurmountable racial differences that do not in fact exist. Next came *melting pot* books, in which racial diversity is present and casually acknowledged via an uncommented-upon sprinkling of brown faces in the illustrations or a casual reference to an African-American character's skin color. Both social conscience and melting pot stories were told from the perspective of the white majority culture. Finally, *culturally conscious* books began to be published, books in which the story is viewed through the eyes of the African-American characters themselves and is told in a culturally authentic manner.

In earlier research, Jenkins built upon Sims Bishop's three-part model to create a model specific to LGBTQ content in YA fiction. Jenkins's model uses category descriptors reflecting pre- and post-Stonewall LGBTQ experience to describe the evolution of YA literature with LGBTQ content using the categories of *Homosexual Visibility* (HV), *Gay Assimilation* (GA), and *Queer Consciousness/Community* (QC).[3] The terminology—homosexual, gay, queer—parallels the historical evolution of the polite or preferred terms for LGBTQ people. A fictional narrative may reflect one, two, or all three of these perspectives.

Coming Out, Being Out, and the Search for Community

Books coded HV include an account of coming out, in which a character's homosexuality, previously unknown, became visible to the reader and acknowledged within the world of the story. The revelation of difference may occur at any point in the story, with much of the dramatic tension arising from what might happen when the invisible is made visible. Like the social conscience stories of racial integration, early HV stories were predicated on a sense of profound difference between LGBTQ and straight people, and the revelation of—and response to—difference was the entire substance of the narrative. In more recent years, coming out is simply one plot element, so a story that is coded HV may well have other elements that reflect gay assimilation or queer consciousness/community.

Books coded GA assume the existence—at least in the world of the story—of a melting pot community of sexual and gender identities, and a character "just happens to be gay" in the same way someone "just happens" to be left-handed or have red hair; their difference from the norm is noted and the story continues. This ideal society would be the equivalent of the untroubled, colorblind world depicted in television ads, in which a multicultural cast of children and adults gather for a picnic, a sporting event, or other pleasurable social occasion. Until relatively recently, teens were assumed to be so freaked out by any depiction of same-sex attraction or an out character that there was little possibility that any of the novel's characters could "just happen to be" gay. Typically, the narrative would come to a screeching halt when an openly LGBTQ character entered the story. The halt might be brief or lengthy, the response might be a smile or a shrug or a fist, the outcome might be positive or negative, but a character's LGBTQ identity could not be casually mentioned with any sense of realism. Unsurprisingly, there were very few stories of gay assimilation in the early days of this literature, but they have grown increasingly common. A code of GA indicates a story in which the sexual orientation of characters is indicated in some way (e.g., a casual mention that David is going to the prom with Matt or that both Amelia's moms drove her to camp) but is otherwise uncommented upon.

Books coded QC depict LGBTQ characters from their perspective within the context of other LGBTQ people and their allies, as members of a community, not as outliers. As with culturally conscious stories told from an African-American perspective, the audience for queer consciousness/community books is not limited to readers from within the culture; rather, these titles are—at least potentially—for readers from all points on the sexual orientation continuum. In our earlier book we asked, "Could these books [YA books with LGBTQ content] perhaps play a positive didactic role in acquainting young readers with realistically portrayed gay/lesbian characters? And could those readers' imaginations be pushed a bit further to see such characters from an empathetic, rather than simply a sympathetic, perspective? Could a young reader not simply feel for LGBTQ people but also with them?" At this point in time, it appears that the answer is a hesitant but ultimately firm YES.

Over time, HV fiction that includes a scene of coming out continues to appear, but the HV "gay problem novel" has almost disappeared. QC has become more common, but so too has GA. Recall the dramas set in war time in which every military company includes one Italian, one African American, one Jew, and so on. In the world of contemporary YA literature, we find sports teams, "breakfast club" friendship circles, rock bands, and other groups in which the characters represent several different minority-status groups, typically including an LGBTQ teen whose identity is simply mentioned in passing.

How to Use the Codes

The codes provide clues to the treatment of fictional LGBTQ characters, but they do not indicate quality. We recommend all of these books. The codes are shorthand for one aspect, which you may wish to consider along with the details of plot, setting, and other features that we've highlighted in our annotations as you make your own reading choices. As the years go by, and new books are published, you can join us in tracking their ongoing evolution from visibility to assimilation to community and beyond.

Notes

1. Michael Cart and Christine A. Jenkins, *The Heart Has Its Reasons: Young Adult Literature with Gay/Lesbian/Queer Content, 1969–2004* (Lanham, MD: Scarecrow Press, 2006).

2. Rudine Sims [Bishop], *Shadow and Substance: Afro-American Experience in Contemporary Children's Fiction* (Urbana, IL: NCTE, 1982).

3. Christine Jenkins, "From Queer to Gay and Back Again: Young Adult Novels with Gay/Lesbian/Queer Content, 1969–1997," *Library Quarterly* 68, no. 3 (July 1998): 298–334.

INDEX